RX FOR ADDICTION

RX FOR ADDICTION

W. ROBERT GEHRING, M.D.

Library of Congress Cataloging in Publication Data
Gehring, W. Robert.
Rx for addiction.
1. Gehring, W. Robert. 2. Obstetricians—United States—Bi-
ography. 3. Obstetricians—Attitudes. 4. Drug Abuse. I. Title.
II. Title: Rx for Addiction.
RG76.G44A37   1985   362.2′93 [B]   84-21986
ISBN 0-310-42750-9

Designed and edited by Judith Markham

Printed in the United States of America

85 86 87 88 89 / 10 9 8 7 6 5 4 3 2

This book is written to thank and praise the Great Physician and His emissaries here on earth:

Mom and Dad—who first introduced me to Him.

Jim Boyd and Dan Griffin—who admitted me to his intensive-care unit and convinced me that His Kingdom was within me.

And *Doctors Helping Doctors*—where I realized that doctors are merely the Great Physician's nurses.

This book is dedicated to God's living angel, Carolyn, whose love, compassion, faith, and understanding sustained me. Thank you for sharing your life with me.

CONTENTS

A LITTLE MEDICAL HISTORY

The medical profession and drug addiction have lived in a negative symbiosis since the ancient Sumerians discovered opium in 4000 B.C. Dr. Sigmund Freud, himself addicted to the "magical substance" of cocaine, touted his drug as a panacea for every malady from depression to alcoholism. Dr. William Halsted, the father of modern surgery, used morphine to "cure" his cocaine addiction and died hopelessly addicted to this powerful opiate. Dr. Horace Wells discovered the anesthetic properties of nitrous oxide (laughing gas) and went insane from its repeated use. He committed suicide in jail after throwing acid in the face of a prostitute.

Modern doctors commit suicide at a rate four times higher than the national average (the equivalent of two medical-school classes yearly). Seventy-five percent of these suicides are caused by alcohol and other forms of drug addiction. In western Europe, fifteen percent of all known drug addicts are physicians. Drug addiction among American doctors is estimated to be thirty to one hundred times that of the general population. Conservative estimates say that from thirteen to seventeen percent of American doctors suffer from the disease of chemical dependency. A Harvard psychiatrist found that thirty-six percent of a representative group of New England physicians used mood-altering drugs on a regular basis.

Unrelenting stress? Threat of malpractice suits? Easy availability and access to drugs? Fatigue? Surely these factors contribute to the occupational hazard of physician drug addiction. Perhaps these play a role.

More important, however, is the factor I call the Doctor-God Complex. We are an arrogant profession. There are few Albert Schweitzers left in this world. We love the status and prestige that goes with the M.D. degree (mine meant Medal of Divinity). It satisfies our enormous human ego needs. We take full credit if our patients get well. We accept full blame if our patients die. We make split-second life-and-death decisions. We love playing God.

This book shows the disastrous results of the Doctor-God Complex and the terrible vulnerability of humans who try to play God.

This book is not just for addicted physicians, however. It is written to every man, woman, and child who suffers from alcoholism and drug addiction. It is also for the families of these unfortunate people, because the disease of chemical dependency destroys the lives of all it touches.

Addiction is a battle; it is a warfare for the soul.

ACKNOWLEDGMENTS

There are many people who, directly or indirectly, made this book a reality. I hope all of you understand that my appreciation extends deeper than this simple thank you.

The book was Dan Griffin's idea—he thought the story should be told. Jim Boyd gave his usual support and encouragement. Carolyn and our good friend Anne Patton typed the manuscript (flawlessly, I might add). Ann Severance introduced us to the good people at Zondervan and offered her very special love, prayers, and support throughout the writing. Roger Borden, Laurel Wilson, and Tommy Loy added their special technical expertise.

Deepest thanks to Judith Markham, my editor, who added class and refinement to my efforts. Any flaws in this book I accept as my own; any genius and inspiration I credit to Judy. She did a superb job.

Thanks also to Bob Brunken and the office staff in 703, Jim Goodson, Tom and Kay Sudela, Jim Hill, Bob Mathews, Joe Godat, Reuben Adams, Bob Hille, June Pape, and Diane Vermersch for their unconditional love and friendship when I so desperately needed them.

And to my family—children: Melissa, Gary, and Courtney; brothers: Bill and his wife, Gloria, and Del. Also, Helen Glass, Perry and Glenda Guest, Sarah Ann Mooney, and of course, Carolyn. Thanks for helping me through the nightmare.

And to Mom and Dad and the people at Cliff Temple Baptist Church—God heard your prayers.

God bless you all.

Rx for Addiction is a true story. Because of the sensitive nature of the disclosure, I have protected the anonymity of many of the characters; the only true names are those of the principals. Also, some personalities and dialogue are composites; this in no way distorts or detracts from my perception of the truth.

RX FOR ADDICTION

Vice is a monster of so frightful mien,
As to be hated needs but to be seen;
Yet seen too oft, familiar with her face,
We first endure, then pity, then embrace.

Alexander Pope
1688-1744

ENCOUNTER WITH THE ENEMY

"She's complete and pushing, Dr. Gehring. Shall I call you when I see a quarter?" The obstetrical nurse sounded calm; her voice had a clipped, military precision.

I glanced at my watch. 5:00 P.M. Perfect timing. "No, that's okay." I shifted the telephone to my other ear. "I just saw my last patient. I'll be over shortly and check her myself. Thanks."

I hung up the phone and finished the chart I was working on. *She'll deliver within the next hour, and I'll make rounds and get home early,* I thought. An ideal day.

Debi Wyatt smiled when I entered her labor room, her face flushed from pushing her baby through her untried birth canal. She was oblivious to her contractions because of the miracle of epidural anesthesia. She knew her uterus was contracting only by keeping her hand on her abdomen. When her hand felt her uterus contract, she pushed. She felt no pain. An i.v. of D5W dripped rhythmically.

"Aren't I considerate? I waited until you saw all your office patients before deciding to have this baby. Better than three in the morning, isn't it, Dr. Gehring?"

I nodded with my widest smile. I liked Debi. Twenty-two years old. Her first baby. She was intelligent, personable, and had taken excellent care of herself during her pregnancy. That made my job much easier.

"Debi, you know I would leap out of bed at three in the morning to deliver a patient as lovely as you, don't you?" Debi's eyes twinkled. "You're such a liar, but I love you anyway. When are we going to have this baby? I don't think I have the strength to push much longer."

I slipped a latex glove over my right hand and examined her. "How about right now, Debi? I'll have to use forceps to rotate the baby slightly, but that's no problem. Let's go back to the delivery room." I left to get ready for what I sensed was to be a routine delivery.

As I changed into my blue scrub suit and donned my cap and mask, I suddenly thought of the first time I had worn a scrub suit—my first delivery. I was a sophomore medical student doing a clinical clerkship in a hospital in Fargo, North Dakota. I had finished the basic science courses of medical school, the "book learning," and was being introduced to the real hospital practice of medicine. My cool and competent mentor was a graying, distinguished obstetrician in his late fifties. He had let me watch one delivery and told me that the next one was mine. (See one, do one, teach one—the standard dictum of medical training.)

I asked the labor-and-delivery nurse to teach me how to scrub so I would be prepared for *my* delivery.

"Well, *Doctor*—" The patronizing, sarcastic inflection in her voice was intended to remind me that though the nurses were obliged to call all medical students "Doctor," the doctor-nurse pecking order would only be established after receipt of that coveted M.D. Until then, they knew more about clinical medicine than we did, and they wanted us to remember that.

The smarter medical students used the nurses as teachers; the others played the "I doctor—you nurse" ego game to their own detriment. I had decided to learn medicine from anyone who would teach me.

"Well, *Doctor*—first your surgical cap. Cover all your hair. You don't want a germ-laden hair to fall into an open incision, do you? The surgical mask fits over your mouth *and* nose. Tightly over your nose, *Doctor.* Your nose harbors more bacteria than your urine; . . . remember that. Now, scrubbing, . . ."

She taught me how to scrub my hands and arms. "Fingernails, *Doctor,* fingernails. Hold your arms up like this when you've finished. That's to prevent the bacteria from your upper arm running down and contaminating your fingers." I held my arms up proudly, just like the movie doctors I had seen.

"So far so good! You are now surgically clean."

"Am I sterile?"

"I hope not," she smiled and winked. "Seriously, no amount of scrubbing could make your hands sterile. The best we can do is to get them surgically clean. That's why we wear sterile gloves. Now pretend—what are you doing, *Doctor?*" The "doctor" inflection was pronounced—very pronounced.

"I'm scratching my nose; it itches."

"You're scratching it with fingers that you've just spent five minutes scrubbing. You're contaminated. You'll have to start your scrub all over."

"But what do you do when you itch?"

"You itch, *Doctor.* You itch."

I went back to my call room and reviewed my notes on delivery. I was ready.

At 3:00 A.M. the following morning, the call came. I raced from my call room to the labor-and-delivery suite to meet my obstetrician-teacher. He was calmly drinking coffee.

"Pour yourself a cup, son. She's got some more pushing to do before we'll have a baby. Forget your socks?"

"I was in such a hurry, sir. I'm so excited! Shall I go back and put them on?"

He laughed. "No, don't worry about it. I've frequently come to the hospital in my pajamas. OB is fun, but the hours will kill you. Are you thinking about specializing—"

"She's crowning, Doctor. We're taking her back," a nurse interrupted.

"Good," the obstetrician said. "I want one of you nurses to scrub in with Doctor Gehring and help him with his gown and gloves. He's so nervous you'd think he was doing open-heart surgery. You'll do good, son. Now go wash your hands."

I put on my cap and mask and began my surgical scrub. I heard the doctor tell the anesthesiologist to put the patient to sleep. (Epidural anesthesia was not widely practiced then.) My mind was racing over the delivery procedures I had memorized.

"She's asleep, Gehring. Get in here, or she'll deliver without you."

I glanced at the nurse. "I'm not even through with my fingernails," my voice cracked with excitement.

"That's show biz." She smiled at my enthusiasm. "Go deliver your baby."

I entered the delivery room, holding my arms up proudly. The nurses gowned and gloved me. I glanced quickly at the delivery-room personnel. Their surgical masks covered their smiles, but I knew I was the object of their amusement. I didn't care.

"Okay, Doctor," the obstetrician's voice was firm but reassuring. "Mom's been asleep about one minute. You've got another three minutes to get that baby out before the anesthetic will enter the baby's circulation. If that happens, we'll have two anesthetized patients on our hands."

"How do I get him out, Doctor?" In the excitement I had forgotten all I had memorized. Three minutes isn't long.

"Mother will help you with her next contraction. Here it comes."

I could see the baby's head distending the already stretched vagina. As the contraction grew stronger, more and more of the baby's head was showing. I couldn't imagine that large head coming out of that small vagina.

"Won't she tear, Doctor?" I asked.

"If this were her first baby, she'd rip wide open—that's why we use episiotomies. But this is her fourth child. We should be able to deliver her without a laceration. But she'll tear if you don't control the emergence of the head. Remember, the uterus is the strongest muscle in the human body. Put your hand on the baby's head and gently hold back. Then let the uterus ease the baby's head out."

I underestimated the force of the uterine muscle. At the peak of her contraction, I felt the vaginal resistance stop abruptly and the baby's head was in my hands.

"She tore, Doctor," I apologized.

"No problem. We'll just sew her up. Now grasp the head, and pull down toward the floor, and we'll deliver the shoulders. No, no, Doctor! Not toward the wall—toward the floor. Straight down. That's it." The left shoulder appeared. "Now straight up toward the ceiling to get the other shoulder out. Good."

The rest of the baby followed quickly behind the shoulders. Amniotic fluid gushed after the baby's torso was delivered. It filled my shoes.

The nurses and anesthesiologist applauded and laughed. The obstetrician, however, was still intent on directing my clumsy efforts. "Hold his head down until you suction the fluid from his mouth. Hold on tightly. You won't hurt him." His admonishment was timely. The combination of amniotic fluid, blood, mucous, and rubber gloves gave a dimension to the delivery that I had not anticipated. He was slippery! (*Don't drop this baby!*) I clutched the baby with a fearful intensity.

"Suction, Doctor," the obstetrician pressed. "If he takes his first breath and aspirates that fluid into his lungs, we'll have problems."

I cleared the baby's airway of fluid, and he immediately bellowed his salutation to the world—a newborn's cry. What an awe-inspiring sound!

I was ecstatic. I had delivered a baby, and he was alive and well. I clamped and cut the cord and proudly sloshed over to deposit my slippery burden in the warmer. His blue-gray color was slowly transforming into a bright pink with each successive breath.

"Good job, Doctor," the nurse said. The "doctor" inflection was still there, but not as marked. I knew then that I would be an obstetrician.

I delivered the placenta, and my obstetrician-teacher helped me suture the vaginal laceration. The anesthesiologist was awakening the mother, and she jerked from the pain of the last stitch.

"What'd I have?" she asked.

"Tell her, Doctor. You delivered him," the obstetrician whispered to me.

"You had a beautiful, healthy baby boy," I replied with an air of competency that I had never experienced before. "Are you alert enough to hold him?"

We talked to the mother for about five minutes and then went to the cafeteria for breakfast. The obstetrician fielded my barrage of questions and listened passively to my adrenaline-induced ramblings about the delivery.

Finally he interrupted. "Bob, you did an excellent job. But you did no more than what taxi drivers and policemen have done for years. You *caught* that baby. In my twenty-five years of practice, I've *caught* thousands of babies. But other than C-sections, I've *delivered* maybe nine or ten. I don't mean to burst your bubble, but any midwife can do what you've just done.

"If you go into OB, you'll find that deliveries will become . . . boring is not a good word, because I still get excited with every delivery; they will become . . . routine. I hope that all your deliveries will be routine, for routine deliveries are a mark of an excellent obstetrician." He put three packs of Sweet 'N' Low in his coffee. "Any taxicab driver can *catch* a baby; your exhaustive training will prepare you for the life-threatening complications. You will avoid most complications because of your expertise and experience. But you'll have to *deliver* some babies rather than *catch* them. No matter how good you may become, you will still have complications. You're going to deliver dead babies, you're going to have severe infections, and you may have a mother die in childbirth."

He noticed the incredulous expression on my face.

"That's right, some of your mothers may die—it still happens. Can you handle that?" I hoped I'd never have to try.

That conversation had taken place years before. Since then, I *had* "caught" hundreds of babies, and I had even 'delivered' a few. No stillborns; no maternal deaths. Complications, yes, but I had handled them well. My practice had indeed been routine.

"Debi's in the stirrups, Dr. Gehring." The nurse interrupted my reverie. Debi's pregnancy had been routine; her labor had been routine. Now for a routine delivery. Catch another baby and go home. I finished scrubbing. No need to worry about scrubbing too long; the epidural had obliterated her push-reflex. The baby would wait until I got there.

I donned my gown and gloves and draped Debi's legs and abdomen with sterile sheets. I emptied her bladder with a red rubber catheter and adroitly applied the forceps.

"Debi, I'm going to have to use forceps to turn your baby's head. He can't deliver in the position he's in now, but don't worry. Forceps do not hurt the baby if correctly applied."

"I know, Dr. Gehring; I'm not afraid." She was alert; her color good.

The forceps slipped easily over the baby's head, and the head rotated smoothly into position. I applied gentle traction and cut the episiotomy through the tiny isthmus of skin between the vagina and anus. Debi felt nothing. The miracle of epidural anesthesia. She gave a gentle push, and the baby's head was in my hands.

"It has girl's ears, Debi."

"What's it really, Dr. Gehring?"

"Can't tell yet. We'll know in a few seconds."

Pull straight down—shoulder. Pull straight up—the other shoulder. "It's a boy!" Head down. Suction. Baby cries. Beautiful. Clamp cord. Put baby in warmer. Routine. Textbook delivery.

I waited for the placenta to separate. Debi and I were discussing names for her new baby. Her bleeding was brisk but not alarming. She would bleed until the placenta was delivered. Then I could give her Pitocin to make her uterus contract and stop the bleeding. I gently pulled on the cord to aid the separation of the placenta. It still didn't come.

"Shall I give the Pitocin, Dr. Gehring?" the nurse asked.

"Not yet. I'm going to have to remove the placenta manually." Not routine, but I had manually removed placentas many times before without problems.

"Is something wrong, Dr. Gehring?" Debi asked.

"Not at all, Debi. Your placenta is just being stubborn. I'm going to have to put my hand inside your uterus to remove it. I like your choice of names. Just think, when he becomes president—"

"Her pulse is increasing slightly, Doctor," the nurse interrupted.

"Blood pressure okay?"

"Yes, sir."

I slipped my hand inside Debi's uterus and, using my hand as a wedge, began peeling the placenta from the uterine wall. Most of it separated easily, but then my hand hit an area that wouldn't separate. (*Placenta accreta? I hope not!*) Placenta accreta is a condition in which the placenta doesn't separate, or if it does, it takes part of the uterine wall with it. In either case, the bleeding is profuse and life-threatening.

I pressed my hand forcefully and felt the uterine wall. No indentation. A clean separation. I swept my hand cautiously, hoping that the remaining placenta would separate as easily. My hand was impeded by an immovable blockade. The placenta and uterine wall were indeed one mass of bleeding tissue. Placenta accreta!

"Dr. Gehring, please tell me what's wrong. Is everything okay?"

Many obstetricians revel in their father-figure role. I loathed their patronizing all's-well-little-honey-you-just-leave-everything-to-me attitude. I had vowed never to do that.

"Debi, your placenta is attached to the wall of the uterus. They are fused together. You may require surgery. I'll try to avoid surgery at all costs, but please bear with me while I get things organized."

Okay, Gehring, you're not a taxi driver. It's time to utilize those years of excellent training. Your childhood fantasy of being a German general has been realized. Your enemy is death. Your enemy's general is placenta accreta. He's on the offensive now, but you have excellent lieutenants in your well-trained nurses and residents. You're fighting on your own turf—a well-equipped hospital. But the outcome of the war still rests on your battlefield skill and knowledge.

First, knowledge. What do you know about your enemy? Tap your memory banks.

Placenta Accreta

Incidence: Extremely rare.

Etiology: (Gehring, don't waste time thinking about how it happened. Get on with fighting it!)

Clinical signs and symptoms: Massive, torrential hemorrhage.

Treatment of Choice: Hysterectomy.

Hysterectomy? I can't excise a uterus from a pretty twenty-two-year-old girl who wants more children. (*There must be another weapon. But first, establish your battle plan: Call for reinforcements, and utilize the troops you now have.*)

"I want every available resident and nurse in here *stat!* Open up her i.v. full blast! Give her one amp of Pitocin i.v. push, and add two amps to the bottle! Call the blood bank, and get her typed and cross-matched for six units of blood."

"Yes, Doctor!"

Nurses and residents were arriving in droves. In less than a minute, the small delivery room was packed with medical personnel.

"We've got a placenta accreta. Her bleeding up to this point has been about 600 cc's. Pulse is elevated; blood pressure stable. We're in good shape now, but things could break loose any time."

I was removing as much placenta around the attached area as I could.

"We've got one good i.v. going, and the blood bank is on its way." I was amazed at the calmness in my voice.

"I'm going to stabilize her and use Pitocin and uterine massage. Hopefully, her uterus will clamp down and stop the bleeding."

The residents glanced at each other in amazement. Finally, a junior resident blurted, "Doctor, shouldn't we do a hysterectomy? I mean—"

"John, she's twenty-two. She just delivered her first baby. She wants more. I know I should do a hyst, and we may end up using that ultimate weapon—I mean modality. But for right now, I can't and I won't remove this girl's uterus. If this were your patient, what would you do? Better yet, if this were your sister or your wife, would you be so eager to cut out her uterus?"

"I don't know, sir; . . . I just don't know. I'm glad I don't have to make that decision." He paused. "I guess I'd wait, sir. There's always a possibility she'll stop on her own."

"Thank you. Now let's go to work. John, start another i.v. in her other arm. Sandy, massage her uterus. Lois, relieve her if she gets tired. Betty, go down to surgery—"

"Blood pressure's falling, Doctor!"

"Don't tell me 'falling'! Give me numbers!"

"Ninety over sixty, sir. Pulse, 115."

"Okay, Betty, get down to surgery, and get a hysterectomy pack in case we need it. While you're there, corner any available anesthesiologist, and bring him with you. If there's none around, get the doctor on call."

Debi was too frightened to respond to any of the activity. Her eyes followed all our movements with fearful anxiety.

"Uterus isn't firming up, Doctor." The information was unnecessary. I could see the blood gushing from her vagina. I then knew the meaning of torrential hemorrhage.

"I'm getting dizzy, Dr. Gehring." Debi's face was blanched. She was going into shock.

"Where are the blood people?"

The technician from the blood bank sauntered in. He was a kid of about nineteen or twenty. He wasn't prepared for the reception he received.

"Do you know what the word 'stat' means, junior? I've got a lady dying in here, and you're on an afternoon stroll. Her blood type is O-positive. Here's a tube for cross-matching. We don't have time to wait for the cross-match on the first two units. I want you to bring two units of O-positive blood here *stat* and have someone cross-match four more units. I want your little legs running—literally running! Do you understand?" He was gone before I finished my question.

"I can't get the other i.v. in, Doctor Gehring. Shall I start a cutdown?" (A cutdown is frequently necessary when a patient's veins are collapsed by excessive blood loss, but it takes minutes of valuable time. We didn't have minutes.)

I glanced at the chief resident. "Jack, find a vein. We don't have time for a cutdown." (*It's almost over, General. You haven't even won a battle, much less the war.*)

"Dr. Gehring, her i.v. has infiltrated." I glanced at Debi's arm. The only i.v. we had going had slipped out of the vein! The fluid was flowing into her muscle, causing a large swelling in her arm. Debi was unconscious. There was not even enough blood in her body to supply her brain, much less the veins in her arms. We couldn't start another i.v. with collapsed veins. By the time we did a cutdown, she'd be dead.

(Nice going, General! Your altruistic concern about her uterus and childbearing capacity just cost your patient her life. General, in every war there are casualties. Did you actually expect to win this war without sacrifices? You should have sacrificed her uterus, General. Any military leader who goes into battle thinking he can win without casualties is naive. No, not naive—just plain stupid!)

"No! It's not fair," I shouted in pure panic. The nurses and residents looked at me, and I sensed their compassion. The blood-bank kid returned with the life-saving blood, but we had no way of transfusing her. No one moved. No one spoke. They were waiting for orders. I had none to give. Seconds crept by like eons in the silence.

"The subclavian!" I suddenly remembered and shouted. "Give me a subclavian i.v. catheter. Jack, get another one, and try hitting the subclavian vein on her left, and I'll try on her right." The subclavian vein is a large-diameter vessel just under the collarbone. Since we couldn't see the vein, it would be a blind stab. But it was all we had left. I felt the collarbone and stuck the sharp i.v. catheter into her body. *(If there is a God out there somewhere, if there is a Great Cosmic Doctor, and if you have any concern about the people you supposedly made, then please don't let this girl die. If you truly control the universe, then guide our hands, please—)*

"I'm in, Dr. Gehring," the chief resident shouted, "I'm in!"

"Good going, Jack! So am I!" I announced. In ten seconds the blood was connected to our i.v. lines.

The anesthesiologist arrived, and a resident briefed him on the crisis. The surgical instrument tray was opened. There was no way of patching the bleeding uterus. It would bleed until we removed it completely. The surgery would have to be done in the delivery room—she'd be dead by the time we wheeled her to the operating room.

I started barking orders to my troops again. "Jack, put on a gown and gloves. We don't have time to scrub. You two junior residents start cutdowns on each arm. We've got to start replacing all the fluids we lost. Lois, put a foley in her bladder. Betty, start prepping her abdomen."

A well-orchestrated team flew into action again, spurred by our success with the subclavian i.v.'s. As I fitted my surgical gloves over my trembling fingers, I was awed by the coordination and efficiency of this platoon of medical specialists. Each movement was purposeful and planned. I smiled in appreciation. "You're all doing beautifully. We're winning, but remember, we've got to remove a uterus the size of a football. That's not going to be easy."

The nurse handed me the knife. Once the cold steel hit my hand, my trembling stopped. I was a general again.

I sliced through the cool skin. There was no bleeding. The blood Debi was getting was being shunted to her brain, kidneys, and other vital organs. There was still not enough to supply her skin.

"Her cutdowns are in, Dr. Gehring," a junior resident proudly announced.

"Great." We now had four i.v.'s running. "Use three of the i.v.'s for blood, and give Ringers Lactate in the other." We could now transfuse her faster than she could bleed. "Let me know when you see the first drop of urine." The kidneys of a patient in shock will shut down to conserve body fluids, so the appearance of urine is an excellent indication of adequate blood replacement.

"Her blood pressure is audible again, Dr. Gehring," the anesthesiologist stated flatly. "It seems you've got things pretty well under control. Shall I send the nurses back to their jobs?"

The nurses looked blankly at each other. Then one replied, "If it's okay with you, sir, we're going to stay with Dr. Gehring until the end, until it's all over. We're all part of this."

The onslaught on the uterus was magnificent. Clamps clicked, scissors snipped, and knots were tied in a flurry of flashing fingers. Jack and I had done many hysterectomies before, but never on a post-partum uterus. In two hours, we held the football-uterus aloft for all to see. Cheering and applause permeated the small delivery room. Now there was just the perfunctory job of closing. We had won.

I thanked each of the staff personally, especially Jack, the chief resident.

"You handled that beautifully, Dr. Gehring," "Super job, Doctor," and other accolades were heaped on me from each of the team. I politely thanked them, but my thank-you's were only a master camouflage of the gut-wrenching disappointment I felt. I now had to face Debi's husband, parents, and in-laws and tell them that a routine delivery almost cost their wife and daughter her life. I had to tell them that she would never have children again. They were thankful she was still alive, accepting my explanation better than I did.

I then checked on Debi in the recovery room. She was sleeping peacefully. Her urine output was more than adequate. She had suffered no brain damage. She would be okay.

I knew where I was going next. No premeditation. Just a compelling magnet pulling me to my office. Life was too hard, . . . or was it death that was too hard? It didn't matter. The drugs would take care of it.

I fumbled for the key to the medicine cabinet. Darvon, codeine, Percodan—my old friends. Too slow. Something faster. Demerol, that's it. Need a syringe.

Now it's needles, huh, Herr General? Pills aren't good enough anymore; going to start sticking needles in your body. Junkie!

"I'm not a junkie! I'm only going to use 50 milligrams, and I'm not going to shoot it i.v. I'm going to take it in my hip."

Does it matter how you get it in your bloodstream? The result is the same. Go ahead. All good generals shoot drugs after a trying battle. Alexander the Great, Napoleon, Erwin Rommel—they all carried Demerol with them on their campaigns, didn't they? Use your head, Herr Junkie General!

"Don't call me General! I'm tired of being a general. I don't want to be responsible for life and death."

Wow, what an ego trip. Who says you're responsible for life and death. Only God bears that responsibility.

I drew the Demerol into the syringe. "What God?"

The God you prayed to in the delivery room, remember?

"There are no atheists in foxholes."

Oh, how utterly clever, Herr General. Do you actually believe that you saved that girl's life?

"Who did?"

God did, in spite of your best efforts to kill her. It's your fault she almost died, and it's your fault she can't have babies, Herr General.

I was crying as I jabbed the syringe into my hip. The Demerol stung. "I'm telling you for the last time, don't call me General. I'm not a general."

That was made abundantly clear by the way you handled that case.

The Demerol was perfusing my brain. I was feeling warmer.

You almost killed her, Herr General.

"Shut up!"

She can't have babies, Herr . . .

The warmth was glorious. . . .

You're not a bad general. You did the best you could. . . .

Thank you, Demerol. . . .

You're okay, General Gehring. You saved her life, General Gehring. A brilliant job of strategic expertise. I'm promoting you to Field Marshall. Great armies will be at your knees. You can conquer the world.

I sank into the euphoria of narcosis.

Debi Wyatt would recover from her battle with death. My battle was just beginning.

THE GERMAN GENERAL

Alcohol

The German-general fantasy was no fleeting hallucination. I had lived with this fantasy since my grade-school days in North Dakota. . . .

In the fourth grade, we studied ancient history—Alexander the Great, Darius, the Roman Empire, Hannibal—and I fell in love with those ancient military leaders. I pictured myself mounted on my own Bucephalus, leading charges into hordes of barbarians, always emerging as the conquering hero. I studied maps of Alexander's conquests—all of the known world. He was my kind of general.

The North Dakota winters were long and cold. Our only diversion was the Roxy Theatre where the plethora of war movies was ample fodder for my young imaginative mind. John Wayne and Audie Murphy. World War II—Wow! I watched in awe as Rommel effortlessly decimated the British. Sly, cunning, and well-deserving of his nom de guerre, the "Desert Fox." He soon usurped Alexander's place in my fantasies.

My playmates and I reenacted every major battle of World War II—from El Alamein to Stalingrad to Iwo Jima to the Battle of the Bulge. The abundant snowbanks were our battlefields; snowballs, our ammunition. We would choose up sides, and I would assume the title of General Gehring. (I was bigger than the other kids.) I used the best throwers as my artillery, the smaller kids as my infantry, the fat kids as my tanks (Hannibal's elephants?). Neither side won the battles, although we would argue for hours over the outcome.

My parents were second-generation German wheat farmers—honest, hard-working people with only an eighth-grade education. Dad worked in a power plant to supplement his income. We only had one section of land (640 acres), a mere garden in the Midwest, and most of it was virgin prairie. We couldn't farm it until we dug huge rocks from the soil. We even had to dynamite to remove some of them. Hard work.

A Leave-It-To-Beaver family? Ward, June, Wally, and The Beav we were not. We were Emanuel, Elsie, and six kids (five brothers and our pretty sister, Darlene), living in a small frame house. I was the youngest. My four brothers and I fought constantly, but we loved each other—and were loved by our folks. It was not a demonstrative love. We were Germans, and we expressed love differently than the maudlin Mediterranean types with their hugging and kissing. But it was still love.

And we had Christian faith. Every Sunday, our family attended the Lutheran Church, where we filled an entire pew. And we had Bible reading and prayer before every evening meal. (*Hurry up! The food's getting cold.*)

At age eleven I joined the Boy Scouts. They had uniforms, badges, and medals, and they marched and saluted just like real army units. The Eagle Scouts were the generals, and I coveted their sash of merit badges—and their status.

I pictured our camping trips as bivouacs on the Russian front. I rehearsed the younger kids in short-order drill. And I added merit badge after merit badge until my own sash was full. When I became an eagle scout, I knew I would become a real general. Admission to West Point became my adolescent obsession.

The eagle-scout award was only the first of the campaign ribbons I accumulated. To get into West Point you had to be a leader, an athlete, and intelligent. So I ran for and was elected to almost every office our small high school had. I was even elected president of my local church youth group and later became president of the regional Luther League. Was I religious? A Christian? No, I was merely politically active, adding awards to list on my application to West Point.

Athletics was my ultimate campaign ribbon. Wasn't a gridiron battle a small scale war? There were logistics, tactics, battlefield maneuvers to be executed. I trained hard. In late August and September, after harvesting wheat all day and hauling the last truckload to the granary, I would sprint across the plowed fields. My boots sank six inches into the soft North Dakota soil; it was like running with thirty-pound weights on each ankle. My Dad would laugh and ask in his German-English, "Why don't you run on the road? It would be easier." And I would explain that plowed fields made you lift your legs higher—thus, better conditioning for football. Dad would laugh and mutter something in German. (Roughly translated, "Crazy kid. Him and his damned football!" Dad swore, but only in German in front of Mom and us kids.)

I prayed before each athletic event. I prayed to win. When we lost, my selfish adolescent faith was shaken. (*God, you know how important that game was. Why'd you let us lose?*) I knew nothing of God's will, only my own. Thus, any faith I had was slowly eroded by my own selfish desire to win. God wasn't there when I needed him. Nonetheless, I added "all-conference in football and basketball" to my application. West Point, here I come!

I wasn't smarter than most kids—I just studied harder. I added "valedictorian" to my list of accomplishments.

An all-American boy? It would appear so, except for one minor flaw. I was an alcoholic.

My first drinking episode, at age fourteen, ended in a blackout. Alcoholics have blackouts. Alcoholics walk, talk, even drive cars, but can't remember anything later. They check their car the morning after a binge to make sure they drove it home. They check the fenders for dents. They ask what they did or said the night before and then feign knowledge of their actions. I blacked out.

If someone had pointed out that I might have a drinking problem, I would have laughed. "Hey, I'm just a kid. I'm just experimenting. Everybody does it. Come on."

I "experimented" again. And again. It was grown-up. It was fun. It was in. My circle of friends condoned it, encouraged it. And we always found someone to buy it for us. Boys will be boys.

My parents punished me after that first drunk. They were teetotalers—absolutely no alcohol in the house. In fear of their Germanic wrath, I hid my drinking from them. And I didn't drink during football or basketball season. But the summer weekends were binges. I didn't add that to my application.

Finally I made the big move: I applied to the United States Military Academy at West Point, New York. I paid my own way to Denver, Colorado, to take the exhaustive academic and physical tests required for admission. I wrote my congressman for the necessary congressional appointment to the school. I prayed for that appointment.

My congressman appointed a principle and three alternates, and I was the third alternate. The principle took the appointment. No armies to command; no campaigns to win; no worlds to conquer. I got drunk.

I was only a senior in high school, and I had already learned alcoholic coping skills.

Disappointed? Drink.

Anxious? Drink.

Depressed? Get drunk.

I got drunk on our senior trip and was expelled from school. The school threatened to withhold my diploma but relented after I promised to make a subtle apology in my valedictory address.

After church one day I talked to the good country doctor who had treated all my athletic injuries and knew me quite well. He knew of my ambition to enter the military and had frequently tried to dissuade me. That morning I told him about my depression over the rejection from the military academy.

"Why do you want to kill?"

"I don't want to kill, Doctor. I just want to be a general."

"General's kill, Bob." He spoke from firsthand experience. He was a D.P. (displaced person) from Latvia who had seen the ravages of the Nazis and the Russians during World War II. He hated war . . . and soldiers.

"Why do you want to kill?" he repeated. "You think what you see in the movies is war—flags, bands, and glory. Let me tell you about war. War is dead babies; war is starvation, maiming, disease. You want to be part of that?"

"No, sir. But I—"

"Go into medicine. Let the generals kill people—you're too smart to kill. Use your brains to help people. Give life, don't take it. Be a doctor."

Why not? I decided. Doctors have status. They're respected; they have authority. In their own way, doctors are generals.

Medicine it would be. Not for any love of humanity. Not for any burning desire to help others. Not even for the money (that just went with the territory). Medicine would satisfy my own selfish ego (not that I admitted that, of course).

Having satisfied the school board with my "subtle apology," I graduated in 1960 and left Washburn to pursue my medical career, leaving behind my good parents, my good teachers, my good doctor. Most importantly, I left God in that small town. I would not find him again for twenty years.

I entered the University of North Dakota as an "Upson Scholar." Only sixteen of these scholarships were given yearly to deserving students. If I received good grades, I could renew the scholarship yearly. A full-ride scholastic gift. I lost it after the first year because of my drinking.

The second year I got a part-time job in a plush motel. I offered an extra service to any unescorted female staying there. I was fired for drunken parties and sleeping with the guests. My high-school girl friend married an Air Force enlisted man; my new girl friend was decapitated in an automobile accident. Everything I touched seemed to die. Even God was dying.

I joined the Army. General Gehring entered the military as Private Gehring. I expected the President to call any minute and say, "Bob, what are you doing down there as a private? I'm sending Air Force One to pick you up. We need you in the Pentagon. Want four stars or five?" No such luck— I was a grunt. I had difficulty convincing the Army of my leadership abilities. I was a private E-1; I even had to take orders from a private E-2. He'd only been in the Army three months; he didn't have a stripe on his arm. He didn't know he was dealing with general material.

"Stand tall, Gehring. And take your hands out of your pockets. Shine your shoes with an apple, slob?"

(*Who is this punk?*) "Listen, I'm not accustomed to being talked to that way. And who are you anyway? . . ."

"I'm your mail clerk, slob. Now get back in formation for mail call. Alexander, . . . Baker, . . . Fitzgerald, . . . Gehring,. . ." As I reached for my letter, he smiled, pulled his hand away, and purposely dropped my letter on the ground behind him. "Harwood, . . . Johnson, . . ."

I waited for him to finish his mail call. My letter was still on the ground. "I'm going to ask you this very nicely, mail clerk. Would you kindly bend over and retrieve my letter and gently place it in my hand?"

"Stick it, Yo-Yo."

My anger turned to rage. I grabbed his arm and twisted it behind his back. He screamed in pain, and I twisted harder.

"Now, *slob,* bend over and get the letter. That's it. Now brush the dirt off."

He balked and I twisted. "The dirt, *slob.* That's it. Now place it in my hands . . . good." Though his face was contorted in pain, he made no effort to wriggle from my grasp. I was much bigger than he was.

"And one more thing, mail clerk. If you *ever* throw my mail on the ground again, *ever*, I'll break this arm. Do you understand?"

He was silent. I twisted his arm again—hard. "Do you understand?"

"Yes. Yes!"

I released his arm and elbowed my way through the circle of spectators. "Ya shoulda hit him, Gehring," . . . "Why didn't you break his arm? . . . That greaseball thinks he's an officer or sumpin'. He's a grunt just like the rest of us."

I knew the mail clerk would report me, but I wasn't afraid. He was wrong; justice would be done. This was the American Army, not the Wehrmacht. I had had two years of college R.O.T.C.—I knew my rights.

I sat on my bunk reading my letter when the first sergeant appeared. I pretended to be totally engrossed. I knew he was coming for me, but I had to appear nonchalant—the other grunts were watching.

All conversation stopped—the sound of giant combat boots thundered through the barracks. He stopped, read a name on a wall locker, and thundered on, methodically slapping his swagger stick on his palm.

Clomp . . . slap . . . clomp . . . slap . . . then the sound of his swagger stick hitting a metal wall locker. I stared at my letter. I read the same paragraph six times. My peripheral vision indicated that the other solciers were standing. Not me. (*That's it—look cool.*)

About twelve clomp-slaps later he was standing over my bunk. I smiled as though I had just read something amusing. (*Good trick—don't let the other grunts see you trembling.*)

Although my eyes were fixed on the letter, I saw my friends motioning for me to stand up. (*Sorry, gang. He's only a sergeant—I'm almost-West-Point. Can't be intimidated by a mere sergeant. Might lose face.*) My eyes shifted from the letter to his boots. I followed the boots upward to his neatly pressed fatigue pants—then to his brightly polished belt buckle. I saw the stripes on his arm—thousands of stripes. My eyes focused on his pock-marked face. He was big—and ugly. His face carried a vengeful scowl, but also a hint of gleeful anticipation.

His swagger stick hit my bunk just as I made eye contact. I leaped to attention. Lose face, who cared. I was scared.

"Are you Wayne R. Gehring?" he shrieked.

"Yes, but I prefer to be called W. Robert Geh—"

"Oh, by all means, W. Robert." A sadistic smile crossed his face. "I'll call personnel immediately and get that straightened out. For the time being, can I just call you Bob? After all, we're going to be close friends."

The other troops were snickering. I thought he was baiting me, but I couldn't be sure. Perhaps the movie version of an Army sergeant was wrong. After all, this was the modern Army. Perhaps modern sergeants were reasonable men. There was an outside chance that he wanted to hear my side of the mail-clerk altercation.

"My name is Richard, Bob, but you can call me Dick," the sergeant continued. My friends laughed out loud. Even the sergeant smiled. He was going to entertain his captive audience at my expense. I was frightened, but I decided to discuss the issue in a friendly, adult manner.

"Thank you for adding a touch of levity, Sergeant, but I'm sure you've come to query me about what happened at mail call. Let me explain—"

"Levity? Query? Oh, no, Bob, I just thought I'd ask you how you'd like to be addressed during your three-year stay in the Army." More loud laughter. "Did something happen at mail call today?"

"Yes, as a matter of fact, the mail clerk threw my mail on the ground and—"

"My, my, my. Shame on him. Where you from, Bob?"

"North Dakota."

"Bet you're a farm boy, aren't you?"

"How'd you know?" I smiled.

"Had some college, too, haven't you? I liked your choice

of words—levity and—what was that other one—queer something?"

"Query." Was he baiting me again? But there was nothing else I could do. "Yes, I've had two years of college. Almost went to West Point, but decided to be a doctor instead—"

He rapped his swagger stick against my bunk. "Shut up!" he screamed. "I ain't never had a grunt as stupid as you, farm boy. You think this is a country club, don't you, stupid? Pardon me, you probably don't have country clubs in South Dakota, do you, bumpkin?"

"North Dakota."

My friends were motioning for me to shut up. I thought he was going to hit me with his swagger stick. He stood two inches from me and screamed in my face. The veins in his neck were blue and bulging.

"Do you understand what 'shut up' means, recruit?"

I was silent. Now I didn't know when to speak and when to shut up.

"Do you?"

My friends mouthed the words "answer him, answer him."

"Yes."

"Yes, what?"

"Yes, I understand what 'shut up' means."

My friends were shaking their heads. "Say, 'yes, sir,'" they mouthed.

"Yes, sir!"

"I'm not a 'sir,' Gehring. Only officers are 'sirs,' and I'm not an officer. I work for a living. Do you understand?"

"Yes, Sergeant."

"You're pretty tough, ain't you, farm boy?"

"No, Sergeant."

"Then why'd you manhandle my mail clerk?"

"As I said, he threw my letter on the ground, Sergeant. And he's only a private just like—"

"He's a private E-2. You're a private E-1. He can throw your mail any place he wants to. Do you understand?"

My ears were ringing. "Yes, sir. I mean, Sergeant. Yes, Sergeant," I whispered.

"I can't hear you, farm boy!"

"Yes, Sergeant!" I screamed in anger.

"And another thing. I know your name now, punk, and that ain't good. I ain't never liked to know my troops' names—it means they're troublemakers. It would bequest you" (*the word's behoove, fool*) "to never let me hear your name again. If you ever, I repeat, ever even touch one of my men again, I'll personally change your ugly face. Do you understand?"

"Yes, Sergeant!"

"Report to the orderly room at 2200 hours" (*what time is that?*) "tonight and every night for the next two weeks—and bring your own toothbrush. As dumb as you are, I've got a job even you can handle." He started clomping away. I was still at stiff attention. He turned to address me. "And, farm boy!"

"Yes, Sergeant."

"Wake up and smell the bacon. You're in the real world now, farm boy."

I could hear him mutter something about "unbelievably stupid" as he left the barracks. After that I was "farm boy" to all my friends.

August 1962. I was twenty years old and still scrubbing the orderly room floor with a toothbrush when Marilyn Monroe died of a drug overdose. But the mail clerk never dropped my mail again. And I carefully avoided the big burly first sergeant. I hated the Army, and I had three long years left.

I wanted to go to the language school to learn Russian; the Army wanted me to learn the Morse code and be a "communication specialist." They won, and I started learning my ditties. Eight hours a day I listened to ditties—dit da, alpha; da dit dit dit, bravo; da dit da dit, charley—I heard ditties in my sleep. Unadulterated boredom.

I stayed out of trouble for months. I shined my boots, said yessir and nosir, saluted the officers, and did what I was

told. It was easier that way—you couldn't fight the Army.
Until. . .

"Will you guys shut up back there—we're taking a test."
There were two classes of about forty men each in one large
room. The sergeant had passed out the tests to our class
and had stepped outside. The other class was supposed to
be studying—quietly.

"Whatza matter, whiz kids, can't you concentrate?
Gonna tattle to the sergeant?" They mocked and started
throwing paper at us.

The hotheads in our class jumped to their feet, threatening members of the other class. The more vocal we became,
the louder they shouted. It was impossible to think, much
less take an examination.

"Just wait until smoke break," one small member of our
class said, "we're gonna whip y'all." At this they started
laughing. The biggest thing on this kid was his mouth. Even
our class laughed at him.

Their ringleader retorted, "There's gonna be a fight, all
right. But we can't all fight. The sergeant will know what's
going on. Why doesn't each class elect their best man and
let them fight it out."

"Yeah, yeah," they all cheered. "Just like gladiators."
Everyone thought it was a good idea. I didn't. At six foot
three and two hundred pounds, I was the biggest guy in our
class. I knew what they were thinking.

"Farm boy?"

"No way, clowns," I answered. "It's a dumb idea.
Someone's gonna get hurt, and it ain't gonna be me. You
wanna fight, choose somebody else. End of discussion."

"But you know they're gonna choose their biggest boy.
The rest of us wouldn't stand a chance. You're in excellent
condition—we've seen you play football." (I was the center
on the regimental football team.)

"Football, yes. But I've never fought anybody." I had had
childhood and adolescent wrestling matches—throw a kid
to the ground, make him say "uncle." That wasn't fighting—
nobody got hurt.

"Shhh—not so loud. Don't let the other guys hear you. You've fought before, farm boy. Everybody has."

"I haven't. I've never hit a man."

"It's just like bulldogging a steer. You know about that, don't you, farm boy? Same thing."

"We didn't have steers on our farm. We raised wheat," I replied. "I'm not fighting!"

"You're afraid, aren't you, farm boy?"

I knew that was coming. I knew it would be their ultimate lever. "Of course not," I lied. "I just don't believe someone should be hurt over a matter as insignificant as making noise. We've made noise many times while they were taking tests—"

"It's more than the noise. They insulted us. They challenged us. It's our class against theirs. Don't let us down, farm boy."

Peer pressure. A human motivating force almost as strong as the physical force of gravity. I wanted to tell them that my loyalty to a class that an Army computer had thrown together didn't extend to the point of hurting or being hurt. But I knew they would consider that heretical. No esprit de corps? Un-American.

I turned to my best friend. "Bill, get me out of this," I whispered.

"I wish I could, old buddy, but you're locked in. If you refuse to fight, they'll call you a coward. I don't think your ego could stand it. If you do fight, someone's gonna get hurt. Maybe you. Not an easy decision."

The other class had made their choice. He was about two inches taller and twenty pounds heavier than I. He had muscles and he was cocky.

"Pure bravado," Bill whispered. "He's bigger, and he's shooting off his mouth to scare you."

"He's doing a good job," I replied.

"You gonna fight, Gehring?" They didn't address me with the usual, playful "farm boy." This was a serious matter.

"Yes, I'll fight!" I said, knowing my fragile ego could never bear the brand of coward.

Everyone cheered and slapped me on the back. I was their "boy" again. Bets were made; money exchanged hands. The odds were even. My friend Bill put down ten dollars on me.

"I'm flattered, Bill, but you shoulda asked for odds. Even I would give you two to one on him. He's bigger and stronger—"

"Oh, but you're quicker and in better shape."

"But I've never fought before."

Bill was silent a moment. Then he said, "You're serious, aren't you?"

"Dead serious."

"Man, he'll kill you. Quick, before the sergeant comes back, let me give you a crash course in fighting." He addressed the rest of the class. "Me and farm boy are going to plan some strategy. Don't bother us for a few minutes." He turned again to me. "It's simple—aim for his groin."

"With my fist? It's gonna be kinda hard—"

"No, stupid. With your boot. You kick him in the—"

"But that's dirty. That's not fightin' fair."

"Bob, there ain't such a thing as a clean street fight. You hurt him or he hurts you. Better that you hurt him first. When it's all over, nobody's gonna say you fought dirty. It ain't the Olympics, you know."

"I don't think I can. A kick there will kill him—"

"Listen up, and keep your mouth shut. We don't have much time. Quit worrying about him. It won't kill him; it'll just make him wish he was dead. And don't wait for him to start the fight. Kick him as soon as you can—when he least expects it. If you have to, walk up to him and say that you don't want to fight—that you apologize for the misunderstanding. When he relaxes and drops his guard—then kick him."

I couldn't believe it, and Bill could see my total shock at what I was hearing. He grabbed my arm. "I'm just trying to save you, old buddy. I don't want to see you get hurt."

"Thanks, Bill." We could hear the sergeant's footsteps on the sidewalk outside.

"Listen up! After you kick him, he'll bend forward and reach for his groin with both hands. He may even fall to his knees. In either case, he'll be clutching himself with both hands. That leaves his face wide open—unguarded. Bring your knee or your boot into his face with as much force as you can muster. Smashing." I could see a glint of enjoyment in his eyes. "Smashing," he repeated. "Literally smashing. That should knock him out and end the fight."

"And if it doesn't?"

"Wear him out. You're in much better shape than he is."

The sergeant was entering the doorway.

"Remember," Bill continued, "if you don't do the things I told you, you'll be the smashee and he'll be the smasher." He was reading my thoughts.

"Okay," the sergeant barked, oblivious to all that had transpired, "if you've finished your tests, turn them in. If you haven't, finish them after the smoke break." He waited for the finished tests. None were turned in. "Okay, smoke 'em if you got 'em."

Both classes filed outside. Bill shook my hand and whispered words of encouragement which I never heard. I was the last to leave the room.

The guys formed a circle in an antenna field outside the classroom. Bets were still being made. Goliath was standing in the center of the circle, hands on his hips, legs spread wide apart—a perfect target. He was smiling, as though waiting for someone to call the meeting to order.

I calmly walked up to him, nonthreatening, my hands clasped behind my back. The deception worked—he didn't know what hit him. I planted my combat boot firmly into his groin with a velocity and force that, had he been a smaller man, would have lifted him off the ground. The smiling expression on his face turned to shock and surprise. The grimace of pain came split seconds later. He screamed in agony and bent forward at the waist, both hands protecting his groin. I lifted my knee, aiming for his face, but he anticipated my thrust and drew his head back. My knee caught him in the chest. I heard his ribs crack as my knee made contact. The force of the blow knocked his wind out, and he recoiled.

He reeled backward, but he was still conscious, still standing. It wasn't following Bill's plan. But as he staggered backward, his foot got caught between an antenna and its concrete base. He couldn't move.

Bill was shouting, "Finish him off! If he wriggles free and gets his breath back, he'll kill you. Hit him!"

I drew back my fist and aimed for his jaw. He didn't have time to duck. The blow twisted his whole body in the opposite direction—except his leg which was still wedged in the base of the antenna. As he twisted and fell backward, unconscious, his leg remained firm. It snapped.

The fight was over; it had lasted twenty seconds. My adversary was out cold, his ribs cracked and his leg broken. The circle of spectators were laughing and cheering and collecting on their bets. I started vomiting.

"Call an ambulance," I screamed.

"What for?" Bill replied. "He didn't lay a hand on you."

"Not for me, you idiot. For him. Help me get his boot off. We've got to get his leg straightened out. Get the sergeant to get a corpsman down here. He needs help."

"Bob," Bill whispered, "let's not tell the sergeant. You'll be in a heap of trouble if he finds out about all this."

"*I'll* be in trouble? What happened to class unity?"

Bill didn't answer. The members of both classes were filing back into the classroom. The show was over.

Bill, my opponent's friends, and I untangled the large man from the antenna base. The blanched imprint of my fist was still evident on his jaw; his mouth dribbled blood. I couldn't stop retching.

"What's the matter with you, Bob?" Bill asked. "You're barfing like a baby. You did good. You beat him. You won."

"Won? You gotta be kidding. What'd I win? The respect of my sadistic, ignorant classmates? Who wants it! And where are they now? Countin' their money. And look at him, Bill. Look what I've done. Will he ever come to?"

The sergeant appeared as we pulled his limp body from the antenna base. "How'd he get like this?" he asked angrily.

"I did it, Sergeant. I hit him."

"Why?"

"It's a long story. We've got to get him to the hospital. I'm going to call an ambulance."

"It's on its way," the sergeant replied. "You men get back into class—I'll wait for the corpsmen."

"Sergeant, I'm responsible for this. I'm going to ride to the hospital with him."

"The corpsmen will take care of him. Now get inside, Gehring."

"No."

"Move out, soldier," the sergeant screamed. "I said move, puke face! That's an order!"

"Sergeant," I said calmly, "you do what you have to do. Court martial, stockade, whatever. I'm going with this man, and you're not stopping me." I stood up and started walking toward him. The sergeant glanced at the unconscious man at his feet and then at me. He was probably thinking I'd hit him, too. He started backing up, then turned and walked hurriedly into the classroom.

"Not a smart move, Bob," Bill said as he followed the sergeant.

"Who cares?"

The corpsmen and I lifted the heavy man onto the stretcher and slid him into the ambulance. I pried his boot free from the antenna base and joined him in the back. We sped off to the hospital.

I sat next to him as he awakened. He looked at me and drew back in fear. I touched his arm. "It's okay. I'm not going to hurt you. It's all over."

He relaxed somewhat and looked around. "Is this an ambulance?"

"Yeah, we're going to the hospital."

"Why?"

"I think your leg is broken."

He looked down at the enormous swelling and then felt

his jaw. He started spitting the blood clots from his mouth. "You're the dirtiest fighter I've ever met," he said angrily. "It wasn't fair."

I apologized to him, but he wouldn't listen. His swollen jaw made it difficult for him to talk, but he promised retribution.

"You'll wish you'd never been born, farm boy."

The corpsman asked me what happened, and I related the whole story. "I shoulda told my class to stick it, but I was afraid they'd call me a coward. And I was afraid of him." I glanced at the man on the stretcher. "I knew he'd kill me— that's why I fought dirty. To tell the truth, I've never been in a real fight before. A friend told me to kick him. Believe me, I didn't mean for this to happen."

The man on the stretcher started laughing, but the laughter brought on paroxysms of chest pain. He smiled weakly. "I've got a confession to make to you. I've never been in a fight either. At six foot five, I've never needed to. I was afraid of you too. I was planning to kick you, but you beat me to it."

"What's your name?" The tension was eased, the animosity gone.

"David."

"Mine's Bob." I extended my hand. "I'm sorry, David. I want to be your friend."

"Me too, Bob." He grabbed my hand and shook it warmly until even that effort caused pain in his chest.

"Rest, David," I said. I looked at my new friend. A nice man. Broken. All because of my own pride and ego. Too cowardly to walk away from a fight, even when I knew it was wrong. I vowed then that I would never hurt another human being as long as I lived. The picture of David in that ambulance was entrenched indelibly in my memory banks. And Army or not, war or no war, I knew I would never fire my rifle at another living creature, especially a human being. Violence was senseless.

The sergeant and two M.P.'s were waiting for me at the hospital. I waited until the corpsmen wheeled David into the hospital and then stepped out the back of the ambulance. The sergeant muttered something about "careful, he's dangerous" and the M.P.'s slapped me up against the side of the ambulance. I told them they didn't need handcuffs, but I got them anyway. To them I was some kind of violent maniac on a rampage.

They court-martialed me. It wasn't a big-deal court-martial like the Caine Mutiny or Billy Mitchell; it was merely an Article 15. There was no trial. The uniform code of Military Justice gave company commanders the prerogative to sentence enlisted men without a trial or presentation of any conflicting evidence. They were justified: I had hurt a man and disobeyed an order. But I wasn't impressed with the Army's definition of "justice." Every time I tried to tell the C.O. about the circumstances of the fight or why I disobeyed an order, he told me to "shut up." His final comment before sentencing was "I don't care if you'd killed the slob, just don't do it on my time. Causes too much paper work." (*This was an officer and a gentleman?*)

"Your sentence is to dig a large hole."

"Yes, sir. How large, sir?"

"Very large—should take you about two weeks to dig it. I want you to pile the dirt very neatly beside the hole."

"Yes, sir. Will this hole have a purpose, sir? Do you want me to put something in the hole after I dig it?" I was thinking of a base for an antenna or something functional.

"Of course I want you to put something in the hole."

"May I ask what, sir?"

"The dirt that you dug out of the hole, Gehring. I don't want holes all over my antenna fields. Dismissed."

I finished my Morse-code training and marked my three choices for assignment: (1) Germany, (2) Germany, (3) Germany. I wanted to see the country of my origin—the home of the German generals I admired. The land of Goethe, Beethoven, Bach. The orders read: Ton Son Nhut Airbase, Saigon, South Vietnam.

Vietnam? There was a war going on over there. Sure, I

could handle a war, . . . but only as a general. As a grunt? No way. I could get killed.

I complained loudly. I told them that I shouldn't be in the Army in the first place—I had a back problem. (*A big yellow streak down the middle of it.*) They'd heard it before. They didn't listen.

I took a thirty-day leave and spent Christmas with Mom and Dad. They couldn't understand why another one of their boys was being sent off to war. They had sent their oldest boy to fight during the Korean War—now their baby was going too. Years later another son would fight in Vietnam.

"Why do they send kids to fight their wars? Why don't the generals risk their lives, too?" Mom would ask.

"Because the generals are too smart," Dad would answer. "Only young boys are dumb enough to risk their lives. Unfortunately, kids make great soldiers—they don't know the meaning of fear."

Both Mom and Dad were silent during that bitterly cold January morning in 1964. The blowing snow almost obliterated the forty-mile stretch between Washburn and the airport in Bismarck. I knew what they were thinking—that once I boarded that plane, they would never see me again. I had tried to convince them that I would never see combat—that my job in the Army would insure my safety—I was not a front-line soldier. They listened but didn't hear. They were losing their youngest son.

I had only seen my father cry once before in my life—I was too young to appreciate the significance of the event. But I remembered that my oldest brother was dressed in an Army uniform and was boarding a train. And I remembered it was during the Korean War. These thoughts flooded my memory as I watched Mom and Dad weep openly in that airport in Bismarck. I felt sorry for them.

Dad pressed a gift into my hand. It was adorned with Christmas wrapping, and I lightly mentioned that Christmas was over, but I thanked him. I was trying to be strong—for them. I wasn't crying.

"Open it, Bobby."

I tore the wrappings and produced a pocket-sized New Testament.

"Take this with you wherever you go," he said between spasms of sobbing.

"Thank you, Mom and Dad. I will."

"Keep it in your pocket. And read it. Promise me you'll read it."

"I will, Dad," I lied. "I promise I will."

"God will protect you, Bobby. You're a good Christian boy. God will bring you back to us. . . ."

I hugged him and held him close, then reached for Mom, and she joined our embrace. I was much taller than both of them, and their tears stained the lapels of my uniform. I found it difficult not to cry—but I forced myself to be strong.

I waved good-by to them as Mom shouted after me, "Read your Bible, son. And pray. We'll be praying for you."

"I will, Mom. See you in a year. I'll be back." I knew I would. I was invincible, immortal. I knew I would return. Once aboard the plane, I placed the New Testament in my bag. I never read it.

The Americans in Vietnam in 1964 were still called "advisors." It was an election year, and neither political party advocated an escalation of the war. War talk doesn't generate votes, an escalation isn't politically sound. But we advisors knew 1964 was just a lull before the storm—the storm would hit after the elections.

The Vietcong knew the lull, too, and they took full advantage of it. They brazenly killed Americans, and we had little recourse. We saw our friends being sent home in boxes. Advisors or not, they were dead. Just as dead as our South Vietnamese allies.

I became cognizant of the meaning of "the Ugly American." We were pushy, deceitful war lords who had little concern for the country or its people. Vietnamese were "Zips," "Gooks," or "Slants." I was ashamed of the American soldier.

I contributed a great deal to the economy of South

Vietnam—my money was spent on whores and booze—but I added very little to the war effort. I did what I was told and kept my mouth shut—as much as possible. But it was difficult to remain silent in the midst of the madness of war. Especially after they sent me from the comforts of Saigon to an outpost called Phu Bai.

Phu Bai was forty miles south of the North Vietnamese border. Desolate. Dreary. The boondocks. The closest city was Hue, and it was definitely not the Paris of the Orient. If we were good, the Army would let us spend the afternoon in Hue. Big deal. Hue had three whores and they all had the clap. If we were real good, they let us spend a weekend in Danang (ten whores, six diseased). It wasn't worth being good. I became what the Army likes to call a troublemaker.

"You're a troublemaker, Gehring."

"I know."

"You know *what*, soldier?"

"I know I'm a troublemaker."

" 'I know, *Sergeant*.' "

"Right." I wasn't afraid of sergeants anymore. Their IQs usually matched the stripes on their arm. They were unbearable.

"I can make things real tough for you, grunt. You know that, don't you?"

"What are you going to do—send me to Vietnam? How about Phu Bai?"

"I can restrict your privileges."

"You've already done that, W.W." The sergeant's nickname was "old W.W." He had been in World War II and stayed in the military after the war. He would fondly remember the "big war" and punctuate his statements with "why, I remember back in W.W. II. . . ." The sergeant never said World War; it was always W.W.

"Sergeant Brooks to you, slob."

"Right, W.W. Listen, don't you think it would be easier for you to say 'World War' instead of 'W.W.'? I mean W.W. has a total of six syllables, whereas World War has only two. It takes more time to say W.W. than it would to say—"

"Gehring, don't talk to me about—whatya call 'em—syllables. You college kids are all alike. You're a perfect example of the men in the modern Army—no discipline, no respect, no nothin'. Why, I remember back in W.W. II . . ."

I pictured the old guy back in World War Two, walking around saying "war is hell" or "this one's for mother." A real hero.

"Don't tell me another of your W.W. II stories, W.W. How you gonna punish me this time?" He had found an obscene poster knocking the Army in the officers' latrine and naturally assumed I had put it there.

"I'm passing you over for promotion again. That makes twice, doesn't it, slob?"

"Thrice," I corrected him.

"How long you been in the Army?"

"Two years."

"Two years, and you're still a private first-class—one stripe. Aren't you ashamed of yourself?"

"Not a bit, W.W. The way you clowns are handling this war is abominable. I want no part of it. I'd rather be a Pfc."

"Abdominal or not—a promotion means more money."

"Where am I going to spend it? Hue? Danang? You've already restricted me from any passes. And a promotion would mean I'd have to shine my boots. No thanks!"

"No promotion and also—what is that?" He walked over to my wall locker and took a large emblem from the door.

"That's my coat of arms." It consisted simply of a large garbage can superimposed on a background of blue, red, and yellow. Two plucked chickens were crossed below the garbage can.

"Explain it, grunt."

"The garbage can signifies what I am accomplishing in Vietnam; blue is for the water I crossed to get here; red is for the blood I will never shed—and yellow's the reason why. The chickens are self-explanatory."

"You're disgusting!" He threw the coat of arms on the floor. "You don't deserve to be in the Army."

"That's what I've been trying to tell you guys for two

years—but nobody will listen." I picked up my emblem. "Want me to dig holes and fill them up again like the last time? Or how about filling sandbags as punishment? I don't mind; it passes the time."

"No, . . . yes, . . . oh, I don't care. Just stay out of my way." The old man wandered off, scratching his head. He had long ago given up on making a soldier of me.

And so I passed the time. I put in my eight hours sending ditties, then my usual punishment duties. I really didn't object to making sandbags for the machine-gun bunkers—it was healthy outdoor exercise. I bought a camera and took pictures of the war. I organized touch-football leagues. And chess tournaments. And poker games. And I made obscene Army posters.

I wrote, too. Short stories, poems, essays—anything that my mood dictated. My friends called me "Ernest Gehringway" or F. Scott Fitz-Gehring" and laughed at my bursts of inspiration. But they liked my writing, mainly because it was generously spiced with descriptive scenes of hardcore pornography.

But mostly I drank. I drank to forget the war, the loneliness, the Army, and the boredom. Especially the boredom.

My hometown doctor had been right. War wasn't exciting or glamorous. There were no bands, no flags, no glory. Only unrelenting boredom.

I remembered his other descriptions, too. I saw the disease, starvation, and maiming that war inflicts. And I saw the dead babies. Defenseless babies with bullet holes in their skulls. Both sides did their share of the atrocities; war transformed intelligent beings into blood-spilling beasts. I hated the Army, politics, and the God that allowed it all to happen. God was not dead—He never existed. The God I had been taught about would not allow babies to be shot.

Once I was out of the service and back in the States, I didn't talk about the war—most veterans don't. But two weeks after I returned home, my father awakened me from a nightmare. He said that my screams had awakened him in his upstairs bedroom. He found me standing on my bed and ripping the ceiling open with my bare hands. There were fragments of plaster all over the bed. I was drenched in perspiration. I apologized and told him that I would pay for a new ceiling. He didn't care about the ceiling—he wanted to know what I was dreaming. I honestly couldn't tell him. I knew it was about the war, but I couldn't remember.

To this day, I still have those dreams. My wife awakens me and tells me I'm screaming "No! No! No!" over and over again. I know it's about the war but, fortunately, I can't remember the specifics. They're locked somewhere in my subconscious.

I entered the Army as a friendly, naive, dumb farm boy from North Dakota. After a year's tour of duty, I left Vietnam a hardened, calloused, introverted, atheistic veteran with a drinking problem.

CALIFORNIA DAZE

Marijuana

For the next three years I pursued a meaningless existence, joining the other restless rebels of the turbulent sixties. I didn't demonstrate against the war, and I didn't demonstrate for the war. I just didn't care. They would fight the war whether I liked it or not. But I did rebel against everything my parents and my church had taught me—"God created man in his own image?" The men I saw in Vietnam were certainly not "in the image" of a god I wanted to believe in or trust.

Instead, I joined the "if it feels good, do it, as long as you don't hurt anybody" camp. I studied hard and entered medical school; I dropped out after several months. I got married; I got divorced. I drank. I gambled. I was promiscuous. I wasn't hurting anybody (I thought).

I moved to Los Angeles to be with other "freethinkers." They were there, all right, and I found them. I went wild.

A female acquaintance and I joined the "swingers" of southern California. This was long before Steve Martin, but I had thought swingers were just "wild and crazy guys." They were, indeed, but they were wild and crazy about group sex—and so were their wives.

Carol and I had gone to a swingers' bar just to see the "weirdos," but we saw only well-dressed, seemingly wealthy couples drinking and having fun. An attractive couple joined us for a drink and, seeing that we were newcomers, expounded on the benefits of uninhibited sexual freedom. We accepted their invitation to join them for a drink in their home.

The affluence of the surroundings overwhelmed us. Their house was on a mountain overlooking the bright neon glitter of Los Angeles. The servants' quarters were behind the house. The swimming pool was larger than my parents' home in Washburn. I parked my Plymouth behind one of their three Mercedes.

"Drink?"

"Scotch, please." I hated scotch, but it sounded classy. Carol had the same.

"I like your place."

"It's not much, but we call it home." We all laughed.

They were young—mid-thirties—much too young to have this kind of money. Must be a Hollywood type—or a gangster.

"What do you do?" I asked.

"Little of this, little of that. How about you?" The question was directed at me, but his eyes were on Carol. I was uncomfortable.

"Oh, little of this, little of that." His wife was a knockout, but the more I thought about it, the more I knew he was a gangster. I wanted to get out of there.

"My husband is in real estate. Commercial real estate and investments." (*Whew! . . . So what's he going to do with you if he is a gangster? Kill you and steal your Plymouth? Or your Timex watch?*) "But I bet you're a student, aren't you? Probably on a football scholarship, with those muscles." She smiled and crossed her legs, purposely exposing nicely tanned thighs. Her husband mixed another drink and sat on the couch next to Carol.

Group sex—group seduction. This beautiful woman was seducing me—why was I feeling so uncomfortable? I knew it wasn't that her husband was putting the make on my date— Carol and I were just friends, so it wasn't jealousy. Was I bothered by the thought of adultery? No way. Married women were open game; it had never bothered me before. It was in line with my feel-good-but-don't-hurt-anybody philosophy, and as long as the husband didn't know, nobody was hurt.

That was it! The husband did know—he was in the same room with us. I pictured him allowing this charade to culminate in some libertine, licentious orgy and then blowing my head off with a shotgun in a fit of jealous rage.

GANGSTER-TYPE MURDERS FARMBOY-TYPE
WIFE CLAIMS RAPE
PLYMOUTH—TIMEX WATCH MISSING

"No ma'am. I work for a hospital-supply company."

"Oh, please don't call me 'ma'am.' It makes me feel so old—but you *are* young, aren't you? How young?"

"Twenty-four."

"My, so very young," she crossed her legs again. More thigh.

"I like your place."

"I know, you said that before. Relax, . . . I'm not going to hurt you."

"I'm not worried about you," I said, my eyes darting toward her husband.

She laughed. "He's so engrossed in your friend that he doesn't even notice us. Don't worry—we've done this before. Just relax. . . . I'd offer you another drink, but I don't want you to have too much alcohol. . . ." she winked. "You know what I mean."

I knew what she meant. I tried to relax. The scotch was lowering my inhibitions, but not as much as her throaty, lusty voice. And her legs.

"Pardon me, I think I'll slip into something more comfortable."

The husband stood up and walked to the bar. "Coke anyone?"

I knew he didn't mean cola—now was the time to

impress him with my savoir faire. "No thank you, we're not into drugs."

He smiled. "No, I meant Coca-Cola. We're not into drugs, either. Oh, maybe a joint now and then . . . as an aphrodisiac. But we find that cocaine and alcohol increase one's desire but decrease one's performance," he winked. "And we don't want to do anything to decrease our performance, do we . . . I'm sorry, I've forgotten your name."

"Ralph, Ralph Jones." I wanted to make it as difficult as possible for his hit men to find me.

"Do we, Ralph?"

"No, . . . I mean . . . well, we feel kinda uncomfortable, . . . I mean . . . your wife and all. . . ."

"Of course you do. So did we . . . the first time. But understand, what my wife and I do is done with mutual consent. After that initial fear, we've found that swinging increases our sexual awareness. Our marriage is actually strengthened because of swinging."

(*Some marriage.*) "But aren't you jealous? I mean, your wife is absolutely strikingly beautiful."

"Thank you. Jealous? No. I'm convinced of her love, and when you get older, you'll find that love isn't sex, and sex isn't love." He poured a Coca-Cola.

His wife appeared in a fishnet minidress and high heels. The squares in the fishnet were large—very large. She wore nothing underneath.

"What's the topic of conversation?" she asked.

"I was just trying to convince young Ralph and his friend to stay and party with us."

"You mean Bob," she corrected.

"He said his name was—"

"Well, it's actually Ralph Robert." Carol was snickering. "Either is okay."

"I don't think young Bob needs any convincing, do you, Bob?" She sat beside me on the couch and put her hand on my thigh. "Please stay," she whispered. "Let's go for a swim in the pool."

"I didn't bring my suit." I glanced quickly at Carol, then said to our hosts, "Would you excuse us for a moment please?"

We went outside and walked along the perimeter of the swimming pool. "I want to stay," I pleaded.

"Of course you do. She's pure sex. I would too if I were you."

"Then let's stay."

"Bob, you and I are good friends. I know how much you'd like to sleep with ol' fishnet, and I want you to. But it's a package deal, you know. She isn't going to sleep with you unless I sleep with her husband. If he turned me on I would, believe me. But he's so . . . well, he looks so hard and cold and cruel. I swear he's a gangster."

"That's absolutely ludicrous, Carol," I laughed. "A gangster! The man's a panda bear."

"Then why'd you give him a phony name? I almost cracked up." She started laughing. "Ralph Jones. Ralph *Robert* Jones. Why Ralph? Nobody's named Ralph, turkey." She was now giggling. "Ralph Jones—how convincing."

I started laughing with her. "I wanted his Mafia friends to have to search for me before they killed me."

At this her laughter became uncontrollable—she almost fell in the pool. "But Ralph Jones? Come on. He wouldn't kill you. He's got a good deal going. He just uses his beautiful wife as bait so he can sleep with young attractive women. Let's go home."

I acquiesced, but I was already scheming ways to see old fishnet again. I had to—I was obsessed.

We entered the house and thanked them for their hospitality, but graciously declined their invitation to stay. They were disappointed, but invited us to a "party" (orgy) the following weekend. "There will be about fifty couples here, but neither of you can come alone. Couples only." I knew I'd be there. If I had to hire a prostitute—I'd be there.

Driving home, I asked Carol, "Did you hear him mention something about marijuana as an aphrodisiac?"

"Yep. Some people say it's a turn-on, but it just makes me spacy. . . ."

"You've tried it?"

"Of course. Haven't you? I thought everybody smoked pot."

"I'm afraid it will lead to heroin."

She laughed. "You *are* country, aren't you? You don't see any needle tracks in my arm, do you? No, it doesn't lead to heroin."

"Will you be my date for the party next weekend?"

"I wondered how long it was going to take you to ask me that. Got to have her, don't you? Yes, I'll go with you to the orgy; I've never been to one. Might be interesting. At least with fifty couples there—I won't have to listen to Al Capone all night."

"You're a good friend."

"And you're selfish and oversexed. But you're fun. Ralph Jones—unbelievable!"

We went to the orgy—the first of many. The maid greeted us at the door. She and the bartenders were the only ones dressed. One hundred nude bodies were drinking, swimming, laughing,. . . and copulating. Everywhere. There were wall-to-wall mattresses.

The women were beautiful. Many were actresses, models, and I suppose, high-class hookers. They were quite uninhibited about their fornicating. (I loved that word—the orgy people laughed when I used it.) There was swimming-pool fornication, kitchen-stove fornication, floor fornication, even pup-tent fornication in the backyard for those who liked a modicum of privacy. (The yard looked like a perverted boy-scout camp.) I pictured myself dressed in a toga, stretched out on cushions on the floor, eating grapes. But this wasn't Rome—this was California. I was living a fantasy.

Carol and I undressed—we were drawing nasty stares because of the clothing. I smelled a strange odor—it smelled like a burning haystack back in North Dakota.

"What's that smell?" I asked.

"That, my dear, is marijuana," Carol replied.

I watched as groups of five or six passed a joint around, each inhaling deeply and holding the smoke in his or her lungs, then passing the cigarette on to the next person. "Can't they afford individual cigarettes?"

"It wastes the smoke, Bob. You share a joint. Want one?"

"No, thank you. It leads to heroin, you know." We both laughed.

Fishnet appeared, sans fishnet—sans everything except her omnipresent high-heeled shoes. "Ralph, you're here! I've been waiting for you."

"Actually, you can call me . . . oh, never mind. You remember Carol, don't you?" She completely ignored my friend.

"Come, I've locked my bedroom door—we can be alone."

"Shouldn't we talk or something first?"

"Sure, we'll talk in there." She grabbed my hand and led me away.

"See you later, Ralph." Carol kidded.

We didn't talk.

Carol and I went to orgies every weekend for the next five months, and during that time my friends at work introduced me to marijuana. They were all young college-educated men who assured me I wouldn't become a heroin addict. I trusted them.

We were playing poker one night, and I smelled the burning haystack again. They passed the joint to me, and I declined.

"It'll make you a hit at your orgies." They had listened in rapt attention to my narrative of my weekend excursions. I was intrigued by everyone's description of the aphrodisiac effect of pot.

"Tell me about it." Not a scientific inquiry—a person smoking pot is not too objective.

"It's mind-expanding. You can get in touch with thoughts and feelings you didn't know you had. It increases your awareness. . . ."

"Tell me about the aphro—"

"Your sense of taste is enhanced—food tastes so much better. You get what's called the 'munchies.' "

I watched as they produced a plastic baggie filled with a dark green substance—it looked like alfalfa. "So that's the drug," I remarked.

They all laughed. "We don't call it a 'drug.' It's merely a weed—a plant. . . ."

"But so is heroin—it comes from the poppy plant. And cocaine . . . from the coca plant. . . ."

"Ah, but that has to be refined and processed—this is just a weed." They crumbled the "weed" on a shoebox lid. They tilted the lid at a slight angle and used a credit card to sift and shake the substance. The seeds rolled to the bottom of the lid. "Can't smoke the seeds," they remarked.

"Why not?"

"They explode and send hot coals everywhere." They took the seedless remnant and put it in a cigarette paper, rolled it tightly, and licked the gummed edge. It reminded me of the farmers in North Dakota—they rolled their own too, but not with marijuana.

"Tell me about the sex—"

"Music—let me tell you about music when you're stoned." One of the guys was hooking up the headsets to the stereo. "I can listen to any composition and completely tune in any segment of the orchestra to the exclusion of the others. Ravel's 'Bolero' is outstanding."

"How about—"

"Time slows down," another friend interrupted. "Five minutes goes by and you think it's an hour—"

"*TELL ME ABOUT SEX!*" I shouted.

"What about it?"

"All I've heard for months is that pot is an aphrodisiac. Is it? What's it do?"

"It increases your sensitivity—your sense of touch is enhanced. That's all I can say."

"Is that it?" I asked. "Doesn't sound like much of an aphrodisiac to me. What about negatives—is it addictive?" Laughter. They'd never heard of a potaholic. Safer than alcohol. No hangover. The wonder weed of the sixties.

By now, all my friends were stoned. I watched them with apprehension, but nobody was staggering or slurring their speech. "It's not like alcohol, Bob." They were laughing and enjoying themselves. In total control. The only thing I noticed was their bloodshot eyes. They had no explanation for that; in fact, they didn't know their eyes were bloodshot.

"Want some?" They passed the joint to me.

"How do you do it?" I replied without hesitation. Ever since I had heard of the "sex" aspect of marijuana, I knew I would try it. Machismo. Virility. Supersex. Why not? Everybody does it. It's "in."

"Inhale deeply, and hold it in your lungs for as long as you can."

I did, gagged, and started coughing uncontrollably. My friends laughed. "Remember, it's much stronger than cigarette smoke—take a lighter drag."

I followed their instruction, and we successfully finished the joint. I felt nothing. "What's supposed to be happening?" I asked.

"Just let it happen. . . . Relax."

I tried to relax, but I was feeling guilty. And the guilt was overshadowed by paranoia. Weed or not, marijuana was still against the law. If I could smell a burning haystack, so could the police. Right now several of L.A.'s finest were probably outside the apartment door, ready to kick in the door and order "up against the wall." I couldn't relax.

I tried to express my fears to my friends, but I would start a sentence only to discover that I couldn't finish it. I would forget what I started out to say. My friends found this amusing.

"You're stoned, man," they laughed.

"But I don't feel anything. I wonder why I'm forgetting things." (Years later when the scientific research on marijuana was published, I discovered that the "harmless weed" obliterates short-term memory.)

I listened to "Bolero" and Beethoven's Ninth Symphony. The music did sound more alive, as if I were sitting in the concert hall. Was it the effect of the pot, or was I just concentrating more? In any case, I found myself captivated by Beethoven in a way I'd never experienced before.

Munchies? I devoured a whole chocolate cake, and I savored each mouthful. My senses were indeed being enhanced—I could hardly wait for sex.

I called Carol from my friend's apartment. "Carol? Bob. Are you—"

"Turn the stereo down—I can barely hear you."

"But that's Beethoven's Ninth. Did you know he was totally deaf when he wrote—"

"What's wrong with you? Been smoking that loco weed, haven't you?"

"How can you tell?"

"You sound stupid, stupid. That's how I can tell. If you're calling about an orgy, it's too late tonight. I only orgy on weekends, you know that."

"No, I thought you and I could—"

"Now I know you've been smoking. You want to find out if it's really an aphrodisiac, don't you? Sure, come on over! But be careful, okay?"

"Sure, see you in a bit." I wondered what she meant about being careful. I soon found out.

Driving under the influence of marijuana is hazardous—my sense of time and speed were muddled. Thirty-five miles per hour seemed like eighty miles per hour. Depth perception was gone, too. I stopped at red lights about a half block before the actual light, all the time paranoid that a police car was following me. And as I crept along through the streets of Los Angeles at fifteen miles per hour, I kept forgetting Carol's address.

Later, Carol asked, "Was it better with the grass?"

"To be truthful, yes, it was."

"I wonder why. Pot doesn't do a thing for me sexually. Maybe it lowers your strict North Dakota inhibitions. Did your parents teach you that sex was dirty?"

"My parents never talked to me about sex. You a psychiatrist, Carol?" I was getting annoyed.

"My, aren't we defensive. Musta hit a nerve. I still wonder why," she said.

I wondered why, too. Why was sex so important? Why would I use a drug (weed? plant?) to enhance sex? Wasn't sex good enough without it? No, sex *was* better with marijuana. And after all, it was harmless, safer than alcohol, left no hangover. (When I felt lethargic the next morning, I attributed it to just staying out too late.)

There once was an elephant named Dumbo who had large floppy ears. Somebody told him that he could use those ears to fly if he would only carry a magic feather. Marijuana was my sexual feather. For years after that, I couldn't fly without it. I became addicted to a nonaddicting weed. As Dan Griffin would say later, "when you lit that first joint, you lit a fuse that would ultimately blow up the rest of your life."

Carol and I smoked grass and went to weekend orgies for months. Carol was the first to suffer the burnout. "I want more than this," she said. "I want more than meaningless orgies, meaningless sex with a Vietnam vet who's trying to find himself—at my expense.

"It's time you forgot about Vietnam and got on with your life. I'm tired of your 'almosts'—almost a general, almost a doctor. You dropped out of med school after three months because you 'needed to find yourself.' Well, find yourself, but do it without me—I'm tired of being a pawn in your sexual chess game. I'm tired of being exchanged for the 'fishnets' of the world.

"You complain about always being hurt when you get close to someone. So your high-school girl friend married someone else; so your college girl friend died in a car accident; so your first marriage didn't work. How long were you married? One month? Two? Just like med school—if it doesn't click after a couple of months, bail out. Another 'almost.' You're sick and selfish, Bob Gehring. And you'd like to blame Vietnam, but I think you were sick long before Vietnam. Good-by." She slammed the door behind her but reappeared seconds later. "And get back to sex without marijuana—you were a much nicer person then." I never saw Carol again.

I found a new pawn for my orgies, but it wasn't the same. Carol was right: it was meaningless sex—no feelings, no communication, no love. And I was tired of it.

I was tired of California, too. The weather was too perfect, too sunny. I missed snowstorms and thunderstorms. I wanted to see large, threatening thunderclouds. I wanted to see bolts of lightning and hear the sharp crack of thunder. I wanted four seasons.

I was tired of the people. It was a continual carnival of transients on their rootless way to nowhere. I was homesick.

But mostly, I was tired of being an "almost." I didn't even have a college degree. (I had entered medical school after finishing three years of pre-med courses—at that time a degree wasn't required.) Carol was right—it was time to get on with life. Vietnam was in the past; I had floundered long enough.

I went home to North Dakota and was welcomed warmly by my parents. They had been worried about me since my return from Vietnam—the failed marriage, the failed attempt in med school, the drinking, the sojourn in decadent California. "Is it true that men live together as man and wife out there?"

"Yes, Mom. And women, too. They're called homosexuals and lesbians."

"My sister in San Jose told me that," Mom added. "What's the world coming to? . . . You didn't smoke any of that marijuana, did you?"

"Of course not, Mom. I know better than that."

"I hope so. What are you going to do?"

"Finish college and get my degree; then I'm going to reapply to med school, but I doubt if they'll let me back in."

"If God wants you to be a doctor, they'll let you back in. You'll go to church with us Sunday, won't you, Bob?"

"I don't think so, Mom. But you and Dad go ahead—I'll just watch a service on TV."

I saw that same look of disappointment on their faces that I had seen so many times since Vietnam. They went to bed, and I overheard bits of their conversation. "Dad, of all our kids, why do I worry about Bob the most? He's changed so much." I could hear Mom crying. "He used to be so energetic, so excited. Now he's so quiet. It seems his thoughts are a thousand miles away. He looks so terribly unhappy." Dad replied in German; I couldn't understand what he said.

I finished college and received my Bachelor of Science degree. My application for readmission to medical school was approved but only after several hours of grueling examination by the admission's committee. I told them that they could flunk me out, but I would never quit again. I meant it.

Mom was wrong. I was going to be a doctor, but it had nothing to do with God. I would do it by myself.

MEDICAL SCHOOL

September 1968, I reentered the University of North Dakota Medical School. The first day of class, I appeared in my ever-present sweat shirt, jeans, and sneakers. The other students were more appropriately attired in crisp white shirts and dark ties. I didn't own a white shirt; I couldn't afford one. I was living on the GI bill and borrowed money. So the following day I borrowed my roommate's shirt. He was a football player and weight lifter, and his neck size was at least three sizes larger than mine. Wearing his white shirt, I looked like a turtle.

I knew I couldn't continue my boozing or pot smoking in medical school. I needed a clear mind, and the frightening memory loss that marijuana imposes was certainly not conducive to studying. What's more, I didn't have time. No booze, no grass, no sex. What a martyr!

We had only two courses that first semester—gross anatomy and histology (the microscopic study of body tissues). Our day started at 8:00 A.M. with a one-hour lecture in anatomy, followed by three hours of anatomy lab. At 1:00 P.M. we had a one-hour histology lecture and three hours of lab. Only two courses . . . great. But the information they threw at us in those two courses was overwhelming. I studied until one or two in the morning to memorize the day's lessons—to fall behind even one day would be disastrous.

Gross anatomy was the big flunk-out course that first semester. The first day of class we were each given a "bag of bones" containing every bone in the human body. We not only had to memorize the bones but also every bump, knob, and tubercle on those bones—in two weeks!

We were then introduced to our cadaver. In high school I had worked for a mortician, so I was accustomed to seeing lifeless remains. But I was still apprehensive and anxious when I entered the cadaver laboratory. The bodies were lying on stainless steel dissection tables. They were completely covered with brown formaldehyde-soaked tarpaulins, and the odor of formaldehyde permeated the room. It soon permeated our clothes and even our skin. We grew to hate that smell, but formaldehyde was necessary to preserve the cadavers.

The anatomy professor stood on a small platform at the end of twin rows of cadavers. "Doctors, the anatomical specimens you see before you were once human beings; I trust you will treat them with the dignity and respect they deserve. We acquire these cadavers in a number of ways. Most are obtained from the state prisons and mental institutions. Others have willed us their bodies. We have a complete file on each of these specimens. If interested, you may peruse these files, but only in strictest confidence.

"In the next four months, you will dissect every muscle, nerve, vein, and artery in your cadaver. You will not only dissect and identify these structures, but you will be required to identify them on tests. At the end of the semester we'll cremate the remains of these specimens. We'll hold the ashes until a member of the family claims them.

"Under no circumstances will any portion of these cadavers be removed from this laboratory. Okay, Doctors, go to work."

Four students were assigned to each cadaver. The dissections were tedious; the formaldehyde burned our eyes. We would finish one test only to start studying for another.

The pressure was enormous. It became a war of attrition—volumes of information versus the learning capacity of the students. By the end of that first year, twelve percent of the class had succumbed to the pressure. What motivated the rest of us to finish and excel? For me it was pure ego-gratification, the need to prove "I can do it."

We had a party celebrating the completion of our first year of medical school. We knew the first year was the hardest. Sure, we would still have to study hard, but we had learned excellent study habits that would carry us through the remaining three years. The worst was over.

Booze and marijuana were plentiful at that party. So were the women. After a year's moratorium, I needed all three—and got them.

The following day I packed all my earthly belongings into the back seat of my car and left for California where I had been accepted to do an "externship" (a summer elective) in psychiatry at a county hospital in San Jose. The forte of that particular psych unit was methadone withdrawal and psychotherapy of heroin addicts. I was excited about working with heroin addicts. I didn't know anything about drug addiction; I had never talked to a real junkie. I thought the experience would be fascinating. But even more, I wanted to rekindle the excitement of the uninhibited lifestyle that only California had to offer.

Before my first group therapy session, I was briefed by Dr. Jones, the psychiatrist. "Remember, you're dealing with consummate con artists. Most addicts who come here have no intention of getting off heroin. They just want to use the methadone to withdraw to a more affordable habit."

"Please explain."

"Okay. The male addicts support their habits by theft, the females by prostitution. When the cost of their heroin exceeds the money they make, they come here. They use the methadone to avoid the terrible withdrawal symptoms. When we discharge them, they're back on the streets with a much cheaper habit."

"Do you cure anybody?" I asked.

"No."

"Why do you do it then? It seems the addicts could rotate through here every four to five months just to get a cheaper habit."

"Oh, we set limits on the number of repeat admissions, but when they reach theirs, they just find another methadone unit. Why do I do it? It pays the rent."

"You mean you don't have *one* patient that is cured?"

"Bob, you've had one year of medical school. You use the term 'cure' as if it really applied to medicine. You think a surgeon who has cut out a hot appendix has 'cured' his patient. Has he? The patient will ultimately die, won't he? Not from his hot appendix, and maybe not for fifty more years, but he will die. There is no cure in medicine, and especially in the treatment of drug addiction. We hope for a remission, preferably a lifelong remission."

"I disagree with you, Doctor. Sure, we're all going to die, but we can give quality living through the technology of medicine."

"I love your idealism, Bob. I had it, too, when I was your age." He smiled. "I don't mean to be the prophet of doom, but drug addiction is such a hopeless malady. Sure, I'd like to cure. But I settle for remissions, and even remissions are hard to come by. Let's go to group."

About forty of us sat in the ubiquitous psychiatric circle. (Everything in the psych. unit was done in circles. We sat in a circle during our staff meetings. Group therapy was a circle. The chairs in the TV room were arranged in a semicircle. I wondered if psychiatrists had circular dinner tables.) No one spoke. I glanced around the circle. Mostly men. I didn't know which were staff and which were patients—they were all dressed the same. In fact, I was told to dress casually (no problem for me—sweat shirt, jeans, and sneakers) because there were to be no "labels" on the unit. It was a "therapeutic community," and we were all equal. (*Equal, my eye. They're junkies and I'm a medical student.*)

My eyes fell on a pair of legs. Attractive. Left hand—no ring. Skirt and sweater—nice figure. Brown doe eyes. Make-up neatly and modestly applied. (*Must be on the staff. Too cute to be an addict. Move on or she'll catch you staring at her.*) My eyes completed the circle. Some tough-looking characters all right. Tattoos, long hair; . . . I came back to Doe Eyes. This time our eyes met, and she looked away quickly. (*Modest, too. I think I'm falling in lust with you.*)

I glanced at my watch. Ten minutes and still no one had spoken. They were going to waste the whole hour. Why didn't the shrink get it started? I couldn't stand the silence.

"I would like to say—"

"Who the ____ are you?" a man with a coiled rattlesnake tattooed on his arm shouted at me.

"I'm Dr. Gehring and—"

"Doctor!" a fat black girl wearing a wildly patterned caftan and spike heels joined her friend. "We know all the honky doctors in this place, and you ain't one of 'em, man."

"Well, I'm actually a medical student." I was frightened and embarrassed. "I've finished one year of med school, and I'm here—"

"Well, whoop-de-do, man." Dirty, long hair. Marijuana leaf tattooed on his forearm. "I finished one year of college; you can call me Ph.D., man." Loud laughter.

"Just why are you here, man?" Born-to-Lose with a skull and crossbones.

"I'm here to observe and learn." More laughter. I smiled nervously. I didn't know what else to do.

"He's here to observe and learn," Coiled Rattlesnake repeated in perfect mimicry. "We're part of his education. Observed like freaks in a sideshow or animals in a zoo; right, *mister* what-ever-your-name-is?" I glanced at Doe Eyes. She was smiling. (*"Et tu Brute?"*)

Born-to-Lose was elbowing his friend. Marijuana Leaf could not contain his laughter. Fat-Black-Spike-Heels said, "Hey, honky, you look like a real all-American boy. Bet you ain't never seen real junkies before, have you? You're a real Jim Armstrong."

"It's Jack Armstrong, you ignorant slut!" I snapped. I knew my face was red. I had lost my cool.

"My, my, my," the group was laughing, hissing, and jeering. "He's a sensitive little doctor, isn't he?"

I looked at Dr. Jones. My eyes pleaded for help, but he was letting me drown. In fact, he was observing the whole ordeal with a clinical expression on his face. I couldn't believe it: he was analyzing *my* psychological make-up during all this. (*Wait, I'm on your team. I'm not a patient; these people are. Help!*)

Coiled Rattlesnake glanced at me. "I don't like being observed, man. I suggest you observe yourself outa here!"

I again looked at Dr. Jones. He wasn't going to rescue me.

"All in favor say 'aye,'" Coiled Rattlesnake continued.

It was unanimous. (The psychiatrist abstained.) I moved my chair out of the circle and left.

When Dr. Jones looked me up after the group was finished, he was smiling. "Learn anything?" he asked.

"Yeah. Never swim in a pool of piranhas. Why didn't you bail me out?"

"Because they were justified. You used your doctor label—you 'came to observe.' You weren't part of the group."

"How can I be part of a group of junkies? I can't relate to those scum."

"Those 'scum' are sick human beings, *Doctor.* Your haughty attitude got you kicked out, and I didn't rescue you because of that attitude."

"I'm sorry—what do I do now?"

"Keep going to group. They'll get tired of kicking you out; . . . they'll eventually accept you."

"I noticed you were eyeing me with a very clinical expression during that whole fiasco. Did you formulate any deep insights into my psyche?"

"Only that you don't know how to handle your own mistakes. You become very defensive. But I guess that's a character trait of all medical doctors, me included. We lack that human quality of being able to say 'I messed up—forgive me; I'm just a human being.' "

He was right. I hated making mistakes—or rather, being caught making a mistake. I remembered the spell-downs we had in fourth grade. The whole class would stand and spell words as the teacher called on us. If we misspelled a word, we sat down. Week after week I won the contest, and usually against Judy Wagner, the next best speller in our class. We would always be the two finalists.

One Friday afternoon she beat me—I misspelled my word, and she spelled it correctly. The whole class laughed and cheered and applauded. Of course, they were applauding her victory. But to me, they were applauding my defeat, my mistake. My face was red; I wanted to cry. I hated that feeling.

Or model airplanes. As long as the pieces fit perfectly, it was fun. But if I glued a piece in backward, if I made a mistake, then I lost interest. In fact, I wanted to destroy the model—it was flawed.

Or the reason why I never tried new sports—if I couldn't be good the first time, I didn't want to play. And tryouts would reveal my mistakes.

"You're right," I admitted to Dr. Jones. "I'm very intolerant of my own faults."

"And the faults of others, too, I assume. But enough of that. While you're here, I want you to get a complete psychiatric history on all our new patients. Most of our patients are addicts, but they may have an underlying psychiatric disorder. And watch for suicidal patients—two of your most important questions will be, 'Have you thought about committing suicide?' and if the answer is affirmative, then follow with 'Have you planned your suicide?' "

"And if they have?"

"Then we watch them. Very, very closely. Maybe in

isolation. We don't want anyone killing themselves on our unit."

For the following three months, I took psychiatric histories: "Have you thought about . . ." "Have you planned . . ." It seemed that most addicts had thought about suicide—"I'm dying anyway,"—but none would admit to planning their own demise. Perhaps they knew about the close observation or the isolation.

The junkies finally accepted me into their group, after kicking me out two more times, and I listened to their woeful tales of self-destruction. During those months of interviews and group therapy, I learned about drugs and drug addiction; but my most important question was never answered— "If you know that you'll get addicted and if you know your addiction will eventually kill you, why do you do it?" The most frequent answer was "Man, you don't understand." I didn't.

I was glad when September came and I could get back to the study of *real* medicine. Psychiatry was not for me. It was such an inexact science. (I had reservations about calling it a science at all.) The shrinks would listen to neurotic patients all day long and offer nothing in the form of therapy. They just talked and talked. I needed to cure.

The second year of medical school we studied pathology (the study of diseases—alcoholism wasn't included), microbiology, physiology, and pharmacology (the study of drugs).

Physiology taught me the intricate orchestration of body organs and their functions. Pharmacology taught me about every drug known to medical science and how those drugs affected every organ system in the body—the side effects, the mechanism of action, the duration, even the chemical formula. I injected drugs into living dogs and scientifically monitored their reaction. I watched their eyes dilate or constrict; I watched their blood pressure rise or fall. We were required to kill our dogs after the experiments—not sadistically, but scientifically. (They would have been killed in the pound anyway.) I overdosed the dogs with drugs and pictured humans dying the same death. I learned everything they could teach us about drugs. And I learned how to write prescriptions.

Each passing month of medical school brought new confidence. Each passing grade brought elevated self-esteem. The "almost" days were over. I was no longer a floundering, confused kid in search of life's meaning. I was a man with a purpose. I was named one of the five outstanding sophomores of the University of North Dakota School of Medicine. I was elected master of ceremonies of our graduation banquet. And I had my drinking and pot smoking under control. It was merely a matter of will power—my will to become a doctor was greater than my will to drink or smoke grass.

North Dakota had been good to me. It had given me an excellent public education, a college degree, and two years of medical school. It had also given me a renewed belief in the existence of God. Not a Christian God. Not even a Buddhist, Muslim, or Hindu God. My God was the Master Scientist of the Universe.

I could now trace the origin of life back four billion years to the replication of the DNA molecule. But what caused DNA to replicate? After all, it was only four inert chemicals arranged in a spiral. Lifeless in itself, but something or someone caused it to clone itself. Who? The Master Scientist.

I could explain the origin of the universe back sixteen billion years to the Big Bang. But what caused the Big Bang? And what was there before the Big Bang? Old M.S.

Biochemistry had taught me about the myriad enzymes in the human body. Some had only one function—they would do their job, then sit back and wait until called upon again. But without that particular chemical, we would die. Old M.S. must have been pretty smart to think of it.

But as powerful as this cosmic force was, it was certainly

not a personal force. "Bob Gehring? Who're you? I've got billions just like you on this planet alone, not to mention the millions of other planets in the universe that support life. I'm out here making quasars and pulsars and black holes, and you expect me to hear a prayer about passing your exams? Come on! I've got things to do!"

I could believe that some Master Scientist had formulated the laws that were consistent in all parts of the universe and turned the crank to start the cosmic machinery functioning—sometimes with devastating results. The universe was the ultimate experiment of this cosmic creature. Our insignificant planet was a mere test tube in the creature's laboratory. And Bob Gehring? Just another insignificant reagent in that test tube.

The Master Scientist had built good and evil into the system. Now it would run its course. After all, no cosmic force has time for details—like human beings.

Since North Dakota could offer no further training in medicine (at that time North Dakota had only a two-year, basic-sciences medical school), I transferred to the University of Texas Southwestern Medical School in Dallas.

Parkland Memorial Hospital was the Massachusetts General of the South. It drew an excellent faculty, and an excellent faculty made their internship and residency program highly desirable and competitive. They accepted only the best residents, and I wanted the best to teach me medicine.

But Parkland had another advantage. As a charity hospital, it accepted a volume of patients unequalled in private hospitals. It was said that a student at Parkland would see every disease, in every stage of progression during his two-year study of clinical medicine. Not only that, but the trauma unit was one of the best in the country— burns, car accidents, stabbings, gunshot wounds. If they took the President of the United States to Parkland, it must be good.

All medical doctors must be trained in four basic disciplines: medicine, pediatrics, surgery, and obstetrics. Medicine is the granddaddy. It is the *total* study of disease processes in all organ systems. Twice as much time is devoted to medicine as to the other basic disciplines. You need to know medicine to know the other three—pediatrics, surgery, and obstetrics. Specialization in these basics and their offspring—plastic surgery, ENT, gastroenterology, etc.—comes during a postgraduate residency. I started in obstetrics, my first love.

As a charity hospital, Parkland's patient population came from the indigent of Dallas County—mostly blacks who were too poor to seek medical care. Hospitals scared them. And especially doctors . . . or third year medical students.

"Hi, Mrs. Washington. I'm Dr. Gehring, and I need to ask you a few questions and do a physical—you know, listen to your heart and lungs and stuff." I turned to the nurse. "It's okay. I can handle this. You don't need to stay."

She smiled. "I think I'd better stay. You may need an interpreter, and with your Yankee accent, she may need one, too."

"Ye of little faith—watch me. Mrs. Washington, which baby is this for you?"

"Six, Docta."

"And have you had any prenatal care?"

"Wha?"

"Have you seen a doctor during your pregnancy?" (*See, we can communicate.*)

"Oh, no, Docta. I's cain't afford no docta."

"I see. Well, have you had any problems with this pregnancy?"

"I had sum clogs a few months back."

"Clogs?"

"Clots, Doctor," the nurse interrupted. "She had some blood clots."

"I see. And where were these clogs, Mrs. Washington?"

"On the bed sheet, Docta. I 'most fell out."

"*He* means 'where were you bleeding from?' Mrs. Washington," the nurse said. "And *she* means 'I almost fainted,' Doctor."

"I was bleedin' from my pajama."

"I'm sure it was on your pajamas, Mrs. Washington. But what part of your body—"

The nurse was smiling. "Vagina, Doctor. Pajama is vagina."

"Oh, . . . I see. Did you come to the emergency room for the bleeding?"

"No, Docta. The clogs stopped, and I ain't had none since."

"Good. When was your last normal menstrual period?"

"Wha?"

"When did you last 'come down'?" the interpreter said.

"Oh, I ain't comes down since my third baby, Docta. Been 'long time."

The nurse helped again. "Doctor, most of our patients breast-feed. Therefore, they may have two or three babies without having a period."

"How can you tell when the baby's due?" I asked.

"Oh, it's time, Docta. I just feels it's time."

"I believe you, Mrs. Washington. Any problems with your other pregnancies?"

"I had high blood with the first."

I turned to the nurse. "Don't help me with this one. High blood pressure, right?"

"Good, you're catching on."

"Any other problems, Mrs. Washington?"

"Low blood with last three."

"How low was your blood pressure?"

The nurse was smiling again. "Anemia, Doctor. Anemia."

"Oh. How about your family? Your mom and dad okay?"

"My daddy had bad blood, Docta."

I let the clipboard fall to my side and looked at both the

nurse and Mrs. Washington. I started laughing. "Y'all are putting me on, aren't you? I mean high blood, low blood, bad blood. Is this a joke?"

The nurse was laughing, too, and Mrs. Washington was smiling at our laughter. "No, Doctor," the nurse said. "Bad blood is syphilis. And I swear we didn't plan this."

"I feel like a straight man in a medical 'Who's-on-First.' Any diabetes in the family, . . . oh, I know, . . . any sweet blood in the family, Mrs. Washington?"

"He means sugar disease, Mrs. Washington."

"No, Docta."

I finished Mrs. Washington's history and physical and presented the pertinent information to the resident. "Good job," he said. "You did the work; you can deliver her."

Mrs. Washington was the first of hundreds of patients I delivered (caught) at Parkland. It amazed me that there were always equal numbers of girl babies and boy babies. The latter necessitated a minor surgical procedure: circumcision. The odious task fell on the obstetrician, and I hated it.

The poor child had just gone through the trauma of birth. Then, only a couple days later, a total stranger in a pajamalike scrub suit assaulted the foreskin of his penis— and without anesthetic. I just knew this trauma would be locked away in his subconscious, only to emerge later in life as some kind of Freudian manifestation—"My problems all started, Doctor, when I was circumcised against my will— and without anesthetic."

And so I always apologized to my little patients. "I'm sorry, old buddy, but your parents want this done. I don't like it any more than you do, but they think you look better without your foreskin. I know you want something for the pain, but it's against the rules. The hospital thinks that since you're too young to complain then you must not hurt. I have to follow the rules—I only work here."

In the instances I recall, the babies to be circumcised were aligned in two rows of about ten each. They were all screaming; they knew something bad was going to happen.

But one particular child's scream was piercing—high-pitched, like a wailing cat—quite unlike that of the other infants. His screams were punctuated by jerky movements of his arms and legs. He looked nervous, if such a description can be applied to a two-day-old infant.

"Is there something wrong with this baby?" I asked the nurse.

"Why do you ask?" I could tell by her voice that I was in for some more nurse-doctor medical education.

"Listen to his cry—and watch his movements. He's not like the others."

"You're very observant, Doctor. You are looking at the youngest drug addict you'll ever see. His mother used heroin all through her pregnancy."

"She did what?" I asked angrily.

"She used heroin—"

"I'm sorry. I heard you, but I just can't believe it. The child is addicted to heroin? He's going through withdrawal?"

"Yep. We're withdrawing him slowly on paregoric. He's already had two seizures. Fortunately, we'll have more success with him than with his mother. If she can't stop shooting up for her baby, she won't stop for anything."

"You mean she knew her baby would be addicted?"

"Of course she did. Even her junkie friends told her to quit. At least until after the baby. But she didn't."

I didn't circumcise the baby because I was afraid the trauma might precipitate another seizure. I pictured the life of that poor baby. The nurse told me he would have neurological problems for the rest of his life. And his home life—Mom prostituting herself for heroin. No father. Crime. Jail. That innocent baby didn't have a chance. I thought about talking to the mother—let her know that her selfish insanity had created two addicts. But she knew that. I would be wasting my time. To paraphrase the nurse, if she wouldn't stop for her baby, she certainly wouldn't stop for a junior medical student.

The nurse was right—that was the youngest drug addict

I would ever see. But I saw the older junkies during my night call in the gynecology emergency room.

"Doctor, I stopped having periods about a year ago and I know I'm not pregnant. What's wrong?"

"I bet your periods stopped when you started shooting heroin, right?"

"What are you talkin' about? I'm not a junkie—"

"Lady, there are needle tracks all over your arms. I guarantee you, stop the smack, and you'll have periods."

Or "Doctor, I'm having such a hard time losing weight. My friend gave me a black molly and—"

"But the chart shows that you're ten pounds underweight for your height."

Or "My father died several weeks ago, and I can't get to sleep. The only thing that helps me is a red capsule. I think the name begins with an 'S.'" Their feigned ignorance was amusing. So was mine.

"I don't know of a sleeping pill that starts with an 'S.'"

"S . . . E . . ."

"Still no help."

"S . . . E . . . C . . . Seconal! That's it. Seconal—a red capsule, . . . you know."

"Let's see. Your chart shows that six months ago your grandfather died, and you needed Seconal. Five months ago your aunt died, and you needed Seconal. Three months ago—skipped a month, didn't you?—your father died—Seconal. Two months, mother died—Seconal. Now your father died again. Your family's kinda death-prone, aren't they?"

My favorite was the cough-syrup ploy. Patients would obtain a legal prescription for cough syrup containing a strong narcotic. (Narcotics are very effective cough suppressors.) They would pour the syrup into another container, fill the empty bottle with honey, place the bottle in a brown bag, and drop it on the sidewalk. They would then show me the sticky bag and date of the prescription on the broken bottle. "See, I just got it filled today and dropped it in the parking lot. Can I have another prescription? My cough is terrible! Cough, cough." They would get a new prescription, empty it, and repeat the process in another emergency room until they had a sizable stockpile at home.

It was a constant battle—the junkies trying to con the doctors. Some of these incidents provided comic relief from the tragic, life-threatening diseases we treated in that emergency room—such as septic shock from abortions.

At that time abortions were illegal and were still being self-induced or done in the back of warehouses with crude, unsterile instruments such as coat hangers. These patients would frequently come in to the ER with the coat hanger still lodged in the uterus. The infections resulting from this butchery were monumental. Not only was the uterus infected, but frequently the bacteria would enter the bloodstream (septicemia) and kill the patient. Tetanus was another constant risk. But no one told these young girls of the risks or complications involved in their decision to terminate their pregnancies.

We treated venereal disease, too. Lots of venereal disease. Primary, secondary, and tertiary syphilis, chancroid, herpes, and gonorrhea. Those with mild cases of gonorrhea were treated with oral antibiotics and sent home. But frequently the gonococcus had infected the Fallopian tubes and formed an abscess. These patients had to be admitted and subjected to massive doses of i.v. antibiotics. At best they were rendered sterile; at worst they required a "cleanout" (hysterectomy and removal of both tubes and ovaries). In any case, the patient's childbearing capacity was ended.

I finished my obstetrics rotation, passed my final exam, and started on pediatrics. Pediatrics was fun (cute kids), but sad (leukemia). I knew I would have to face cancer in all specialties of medicine, but I couldn't handle the deaths of small children. It was a depressing rotation.

Medicine was next. After months of examining crying kids, I welcomed the opportunity to examine a patient who didn't kick me. One of our responsibilities on this duty was to draw all the blood samples and start all the i.v.'s on the patients on our ward. We became proficient in finding veins, cannulating them, and filling our syringes with copious quantities of their hemal fluids. (Believe me, bloodletting is still practiced in modern medicine, but now only for diagnostic reasons.)

Finding a vein in fat people was difficult; in drug addicts, it was impossible. Their veins were so scarred by repeated injections that they felt like subcutaneous ropes. I soon learned to tell the addicts how much blood I needed, give them the syringe and the tubes, leave the room, and let them draw their own blood. When I returned, the blood samples were always ready for me. They knew where the good veins were, and they knew how to draw their own blood. However, I always made a point of retrieving the syringe.

Alcoholics presented a different problem or problems. They were usually so emaciated from a diet of straight alcohol that their veins stuck out prominently. Drawing blood was easy. But the medical problems resulting from their alcoholism were so immense that we dreaded having a drunk assigned to us. Sick drunks meant hard work. Sick drunks meant sleepless nights. And we all knew our life-saving efforts were futile. As soon as the patient was "toned up" (cured of his crisis), he would get drunk again and return with another life-threatening complication.

The d.t.'s were the most life-threatening emergencies. Acute withdrawal of alcohol frequently precipitated the hallucinations and convulsions of delirium tremens. We used the "string sign" to determine impending d.t.'s. For this, we would hold an imaginary string between the fingers of both hands and ask the patient to tell us the color of the string. If he replied that there was no string, we breathed easy. But more often than not we got a "positive string sign" (the patient told us the color of the nonexistent string). We would then give him Valium to cool down his hyperactive central nervous system.

But the task we dreaded most was the treatment of bleeding esophageal varices. This complication would occur when an alcoholic's markedly enlarged liver acted as a dam to the flow of blood in the abdomen. The backed up blood swelled the veins of the esophagus until they burst, and the patient vomited blood. He would bleed to death unless we stemmed the crimson tide. Method? Ice water down his gullet.

And so we'd stay up all night pushing the cold water over bleeding veins in his esophagus. If we withdrew the water and it was bloody, we'd do it again. And again. Until the bleeding stopped, and that took hours. We were sleepy med students doing boring work, and we cursed our drunken patients because we knew they'd return in a week with the same bleeding veins. All because they couldn't stop drinking. Where was their will power?

Fortunately the boredom of treating esophageal varices was more than compensated for by the excitement of treating the exotic diseases that plagued the patients of Parkland Hospital. We had studied these strange maladies and would probably never see them in private practice, but they were abundant at Parkland. But nothing was more exciting than the surgical trauma rotation during my senior year.

As medical students we scrubbed in on the big-time surgery: knife and gunshot wounds, lacerated livers, and ruptured spleens. But in surgery we only held retractors; we never got to operate. The excitement came in the emergency room when we were getting the patient stable enough to withstand the surgical assault. Many never made it into the emergency room (D.O.A.'s) and many more never made it out. The human body can only withstand so much trauma. But I was amazed at how much it can withstand. I would hear myself whisper, "Ain't no way we're going to save this one," only to find that, miraculously, the patient lived.

The ER was a zoo on Friday and Saturday nights. Weekend parties with their inherent drunkenness caused car accidents. Alcohol also caused arguments, and arguments were settled with knives or guns or pool cues or human teeth. As senior medical students, we got all the experience we wanted. Sure, the serious surgery was done by the residents while we held retractors, but we sutured the nonpenetrating lacerations. And there were more than enough for everyone.

The drug overdoses, if they were still alive, were sent to ICU. Most came in D.O.A., with needles still stuck in their arms and foam bubbling from their mouths and nostrils. (They died in pulmonary edema—fluid in their lungs—thus the foam.) One D.O.A. had a gold ring through his nose; his nasal septum had been eaten away by cocaine. Cause of death: stroke. He had injected cocaine, and his already elevated blood pressure was pushed sky-high by the coke. An artery in his brain ruptured under the pressure. The coke literally blew his brains out.

During slack times (there were a few) I drank coffee in Trauma Room One, the room where John Kennedy died. One evening I found myself imagining the excitement and fear that the doctors must have felt on that November day in 1963—i.v.'s were started, X-rays done, lab tests collected. I wondered if their treatment was different because he was the President of the United States. I wondered how they felt when death finally won. . . .

"Gehring, we need you to restrain a patient in Trauma Room Two. Knife wound—drunk and drugged—he's wrecking the place, and he won't hold still long enough to get an i.v. started. He's already hit a nurse. . . ."

I followed the other medical student into the room. The nurses were cowering in the corner; the floor was littered with broken i.v. bottles. The patient was sitting on the table with one hand held over a fourteen inch knife wound in his abdomen. Each breath pushed his intestines out of the wound; they coiled around his bloody fingers like a snake.

He was frantically trying to push his guts back through the wound. Blood was dripping from the table. His eyes showed stark animal terror.

"You're trying to kill me. Stay away," he shouted. His shouting only pushed more of the bloody intestine through the wound.

"We're trying to help you—you're in a hospital—"

"Forget it, Gehring," the other student interrupted. "We've tried reasoning with him. We can't even get close enough to sedate him. By rights, he shouldn't even be alive, much less awake. I suppose we can wait until he passes out from blood loss—"

"No way. I'm going to rush him and hold his arms while you get an i.v. going—okay?"

I was behind the patient before the other student could answer. I reached for his free arm and didn't see the elbow that caught me across the jaw and sent me sprawling into a stack of empty oxygen tanks. I was like a bowling ball—the tanks scattered in all directions. The noise was deafening. (Where's he getting his strength? A normal man would be dead.)

The chief resident in surgery appeared in the doorway holding a large syringe. He was a burly man with a barrel chest. He looked at me in the center of the oxygen tanks and smiled, then addressed our belligerent patient.

"Oh, Mr. Alexander, you're still alive, I see. I hear you have the strength of ten men. Could it be the large amount of drugs you've taken recently?"

"Stay away from me—"

"Shut up, Mr. Alexander," the resident continued calmly. "I hold in my hand a rather large syringe, as you can see. It is filled with acid—no, not the LSD acid that you like so much, but sulphuric acid. It'll eat a hole through you in a split second. I save it for all my patients who find it necessary to hit my nurses." He glanced at me and grinned. "You can hit the med students, but the nurses are off-limits. And I guarantee that if you open your mouth again, or if you don't do what I tell you, I'll stick this needle right in your eye." We all winced. "Do you understand?" He waved the syringe in front of the man's face.

"Yes, sir."

"Good. Now let me explain my game plan to you. You are dying. One of your cohorts has split you from stem to stern, and in case you didn't know, you're holding your guts in your hand. Without surgery, you've got about two minutes to live. That big medical student sitting in the oxygen tanks is going to start an i.v. on you, and you're going to let him. Then we'll transfuse some of the blood you've lost, take you to surgery, and put you back together. Okay?"

The patient stared at the syringe and fell back on the table. He was now too weak to fight. I started the i.v. as the nurses cut his clothing with a pair of scissors. We had him prepped and in the operating room in ninety seconds.

I watched the chief resident put the syringe of sulphuric acid in his lab coat pocket as we scrubbed for surgery. "Aren't you afraid it will leak and burn a hole in your coat?" I asked.

He laughed. "It's only lemonade. I carry it with me in case I'm in surgery for four or five hours. The circulating nurses just stick it through my face mask and squirt some into my mouth. But to "scumbag" in there it was sulphuric acid. Highly effective."

We spent the next five hours putting "scumbag" back together. I knew the chief resident disliked this patient, but personalities played no role in the operating room. We stayed up all night saving the life of a patient who would probably burglarize our homes after discharge. It didn't matter. Death was our enemy.

Of all the lessons Parkland taught me, I think that was the most important. I listened to the complaints of the Highland Park socialites who had to wait hours for a doctor to suture a minor laceration. "I told the ambulance driver to take me to a private hospital. Instead he brought me here . . . with *these* people." They didn't understand that their laceration could wait—there was a "scumbag" who was dying, and he got top billing.

John Kennedy got the best the hospital had to offer, but not because he was President. It was because he was dying.

June 5, 1972. Graduation. Dallas was hot and humid. Thunderclouds formed over the city skyline.

"Good night for a tornado," Mom said. She always liked to talk about the weather.

"Good night for a hatchet murder," brother Bill replied.

We all laughed, and I said, "Mom, have you noticed that the more education your kids get, the weirder their sense of humor becomes?"

"That's okay—we're proud of all our children—weird or not."

They had reason to be proud. My sister was happily married and raising two delightful children. All my brothers had college degrees, and I was the third son to receive the doctor of medicine degree. (Bill had specialized in pathology, and Del, OB-Gyn.)

"Who'da ever thunk? Four years ago I couldn't even spell doctor, and now I are one."

"I'll believe it when I see your diploma," the oldest Dr. Gehring replied.

I agreed. It did seem unbelievable. Four years of grueling study, sleepless nights, punishing exams. Four years of borrowed money, hamburgers and bologna sandwiches, and a banged-up Opel without a heater.

I listened to the keynote speaker tell us about our role in the future of medicine. We recited the Oath of Hippocrates: "I swear by Apollo . . ." and I received my diploma:

The University of Texas
Southwestern Medical School at Dallas
Has conferred on
Wayne Robert Gehring
the degree of
Doctor of Medicine

With all the rights, privileges and honors, as well as the obligations and responsibilities pertaining to that degree.

It was time to enjoy the rights, privileges, and honors.

Friends at my apartment complex gave a party in my honor. Champagne punch, white tablecloths, catered food—for me! I was no longer an "almost." I was a medical doctor. I was a somebody.

I got high with a little help from my friends. Blackout high. They said I fell into the pool with my clothes on. . . .

INTERN ON CALL

"Are you the intern on call?" The nurse's heavy oriental accent was hard to decipher. I squinted at the clock. 4:00 A.M. I had been asleep exactly twenty minutes.

"Am I what?" I mumbled into the phone.

"Are you the intern on call?" she repeated emphatically.

"I'm Dr. Gehring, and yes, I happen to be on call."

"You have to come to room 5477 and pronounce a patient dead."

"Right. Sure. Be right over." Click. I rolled over and pulled the blanket over my shoulders. Fat chance. Heart attack, yes. Hypovolemic shock, yes. But to interrupt my allotted ninety-minute slumber for a dead man—no way. He's dead. I can't help him.

At 4:15 A.M. the phone rang again. Same oriental accent. "Are you coming, Doctor?"

"Nurse, I will be there when I get there! And don't call back!" I slammed the receiver down and went back to sleep.

4:25 A.M. Different voice on the phone. Angry, but at least she spoke English. "Who is this?" she shouted.

"Who were you calling?" I replied calmly.

"Don't get smart with me, Doctor. Are you the intern on call?"

"I'm Dr. Gehring, and yes, . . . oh, never mind. Whatdya want?"

"I'm the nursing supervisor on five, and Miss Foo tells

me she's called you twice to pronounce a patient dead, and you won't come." Still angry.

"I'm sorry, I didn't get your name." I was too tired to shout back at her.

"My name doesn't matter. Are you coming or not?"

"Well, Miss Supervisor, is the patient in fact dead?"

"Of course he is."

"You've listened for a heart beat, checked for spontaneous respirations, got a flat EKG and no brain waves?"

"No, I haven't done all that! He's cold. His body is at room temperature. He's dead, any idiot can tell that."

"Obviously." (*You did.*)

Silence.

"What I'm trying to say, Miss Supervisor—"

"Mrs. Crawford." Her voice was softening, but not much.

"Mrs. Crawford, what I'm trying to say is this: From your description, the man appears to be dead, deceased, passed on, gone-to-see-his-maker. He is no more. Why do you need me? You just pronounce him dead yourself, and get on with your work, and I'll get back to sleep."

"You smartass interns are all alike—"

"Please, Mrs. Crawford, your language." As tired as I was, I enjoyed the banter. After years of being a whipping-boy med student, I relished my first opportunity to reverse the pecking order.

"Okay, *Doctor*. Let me put it to you as bluntly as I can. It is now July third. You've been an intern for three whole days. You have no earthly idea of how a hospital operates. I can't pronounce him dead, because I'm not a doctor—"

"That's abundantly clear, Mrs. Crawford."

"Don't interrupt me." She was shouting again. "I've got to get him out of that room to get it cleaned up for another patient. Do you understand?" Her voice cracked, and her breath was coming in short staccato bursts.

"Mrs. Crawford," I replied as softly as I could, knowing that would infuriate her even more, "let me put it to you as bluntly as I can. I've been up for . . ." I glanced at my watch, "twenty-two hours and forty-two minutes. In another thirty minutes I'll have to get up again. I'm tired, very tired. I've spent most of my sleep time arguing with you and Miss Fung—"

"Foo, her name is Miss Foo."

"Foo, Fung, Dung, whatever. The point is, your patient is dead, and I'm alive. But I won't be unless I get some sleep. If cleaning your little hospital room rates such a high priority with you, I suggest that you move your dead patient to the morgue, and I'll pronounce him dead down there *after* I get some sleep. Or stick him out in the hall, and clean your room. Or stick him in a closet. In fact, Mrs. Crawford, after talking with you, I know a perfect place you can stick him while you clean your room. Do I make myself clear?"

"That does it, Doctor. I'm writing an incident report on you!"

"What's an incident report?"

"You'll find out, stupid!" Click.

(*Aren't you ashamed of yourself, Gehring? In the time you spent playing power games with that nurse, you could have pronounced him dead and been back asleep. Had to exert the muscle of that M.D., didn't you?*) I rolled over and went to sleep.

Thirty minutes later the alarm went off. For a period of time I didn't know where I was. There was only that shrill buzz that I had to quiet. I opened my eyes to find the source of that aggravation, and only then realized I was in a hospital call room, that I was a doctor who had to get up and go back to work. I fantasized about going back to sleep, but then remembered two of the eleven patients I had admitted the previous evening. Both were in congestive heart failure and needed a lot of "toning up."

I rolled lazily out of bed, shuffled to the washbasin, and began splashing my face with cold water. I did that whenever I was sleepy, thinking that it would wake me up. It never did. It just made me a sleepy man with a cold face.

First I went to 5477 to see the dead man. He was still

there and still dead. I decided not to listen for heart sounds and check for respiration. He was blue and cold and obviously dead. I started to leave the room, and then I remembered stories of patients awakening in the morgue after a doctor had pronounced them dead when, in fact, they were very much alive. It would be rather embarrassing for me to send a living patient to the morgue. Not a good way to start my medical career.

Alone in that dimly lit room with the dead man, I felt nervous and uncomfortable. I had seen many dead people before and had always felt the same queasy, uneasy feeling. I guess the musty smell of death reminded me of my mortality.

The man's eyes were open, and he stared unflinchingly at the ceiling. His cheeks were hollow, and his mouth was caught in a sardonic smile. I grabbed his hand and immediately drew back. He was so cold, so very cold. "Sir, if you're alive, just tell me, and we can stop this whole ordeal." I laughed at myself, . . . talking to a dead man!

I hurriedly fished my stethoscope and mirror out of my bag. I placed the mirror under his nostrils and watched for mist to appear. A voice in my mind told me not to look into his eyes. The more persistent the voice became, the more compelled I was to look. I did, and that deathly stare burned through me. I tried closing his eyelids, but the lids kept popping open.

There was no mist on the mirror. He was not breathing. I placed the stethoscope directly over his heart—nothing. I threw the tools in the bag and ran for the door. I felt his macabre stare following me. I slammed the door behind me.

I regained my composure as I walked to the nurses' station. I checked the nametags of the nurses. Miss Foo and Mrs. Crawford were busy discussing some form they were filling out. Mrs. Crawford kept saying "What?" to Miss Foo— she couldn't understand her either.

Mrs. Crawford looked exactly as I had pictured her.

Typical nursing supervisor. Late fifties. Blue hair. (*Why don't they leave their hair gray?*) Dour expression.

"Mrs. Crawford, you're right. Your patient is dead. I'll just jot a note on his chart and get out of your hair." (*Had I said "your blue hair"?*) I glanced over her shoulder at the form she was filling out. INCIDENT REPORT. "You can clean your room now, Mrs. Crawford."

She didn't acknowledge my presence. Just kept on writing.

"There," she finally spoke to Miss Foo, "it's all in the incident report."

"Would someone please tell me what an incident report is?" I asked. The other nurses just smiled and continued working. I left to start my rounds.

Two days later I heard my name being paged over the hospital intercom. "Dr. Gehring, Dr. Robert Gehring." I felt important. I called the page operator. "Dr. Gehring, you are to call Susan, Dr. Sparks' secretary, at 2471." Important? No way! I was in trouble. Sparks was the chief of the service.

"Susan? Dr. Gehring. I'm supposed to call you."

"Dr. Gehring? Let's see, . . . oh, yes, here it is. You're supposed to be in Dr. Sparks' office at two o'clock this afternoon to discuss an incident report."

"Susan, for heaven's sake, tell me what is an incident report? That's all I've heard for days."

Her voice betrayed a smile. "Dr. Sparks will tell you. In your case, it's no big deal. I admire you. Most interns take a full month to get an incident report. You set a record—only three days. Relax. Dr. Sparks is a nice man. See you at two."

I was in his waiting room at 1:45, not-reading a National Geographic. At 2:00 Susan ushered me into Dr. Sparks' office. She winked at me as she left. Her wink was no solace.

Dr. Sparks was as impressive as his office. Not intimidating, but impressive. Gray hair, tailor-made suit, diamond tie tack, Rolex watch, manicured fingernails. His walls were plastered with plaques and awards. I was speechless.

"Sit down, Bob." He sucked on his Dunhill pipe. "I've

been perusing your file . . . impressive." (*I always like a man who uses the word peruse.*)

"Eagle scout," he continued, "valedictorian, Upson scholar, Vietnam veteran, selected as one of five outstanding sophomores in your med-school class, good recommendations. . . ." (*That's it, always build a man up before you tear him down.*)

"Impressive, very impressive. Now, it appears that a Mrs. Crawford . . ." (*Here it comes.*) "and a Miss Fung—"

"Foo, sir."

"I beg your pardon?"

"Foo, sir. I think the nurse's name is Foo."

He glanced at his report. "Oh, yes, of course, you're right. Foo, Fung, whatever. In any case, these nurses state that they called you three times to pronounce a patient dead and that you adamantly refused to get out of bed. Is that correct?"

"Yes, sir."

"Mrs. Crawford further states that you told her she could take the dead man and stick him up her . . ." He again glanced at his report. "It says here 'an unmentionable orifice of her lower gastrointestinal tract'; is that correct?"

"That was only implied, sir. I wouldn't say that to anyone."

"Of course not, nor would I."

I wanted to laugh, and he was doing his best to repress a smile.

"You've never had an incident report, have you? Of course not, how could you. You've only been here . . . my, my, you got one after only three days. I think that's a record."

"Yes, sir."

"Well, let's talk doctor to doctor." He leaned forward and tapped his Dunhill on his palm. "I'm flooded with incident reports every July when the new interns start. They're mostly concerning verbal altercations between nurses and my new doctors. The interns are proud of that new M.D., and they like to throw their weight around. I want you to be proud of that degree, Bob, but I also want you to be smart.

"The nurses run the hospital. They always have and they always will. We doctors only work here. If you fight them, they'll make life miserable for you. They'll call you for laxative orders and sleeping pill orders when you're trying to get a few hours' sleep—just because they don't like you. But if you make friends with them, they'll let you sleep. They'll handle a lot of your scut work for you. Make it easy on yourself; be smart. Let the nurses work for you. You'll have more time for the important things. Am I making any sense?"

"Yes, sir. Very much." I replied. "Thank you."

"So much for that. I'd suggest you go apologize to Mrs. Crawford. I know Mrs. Crawford; she's been around for years. Good nurse, . . . or at least she used to be. Make friends with her. Appeal to her female vanity. Compliment her on her hair—"

"But it's blue, sir."

"Blue?"

"Yes, sir."

"I wonder why they do that!" He refilled his pipe. "Well, compliment her on something—you know what I mean."

"Yes, sir."

"And say something to Miss Fung—"

"Foo."

"Who?"

"Foo, sir."

"Oh, yes, Foo. Say something to her too. Three days, that's remarkable. . . . Well, you better get back to work." He rose and walked to the door. "And Bob, . . ."

"Yes, sir?"

"No more incident reports, okay?"

"Yes, sir. Thank you, sir." I followed him into his waiting room. "Oh, Dr. Sparks, one question, if I may. How long will I be the intern on call? Do the nurses ever start calling us by our names? Will I ever be Doctor Gehring?"

"Only when you *become* Doctor Gehring, Bob. There are some interns who remain the IOC their full year of internship. The nurses are very perceptive; they'll call you 'Doctor' when you are one. You'll know when you've arrived. Have a good internship."

The following morning I took Miss Foo and Mrs. Crawford to breakfast. Whatever deficiencies Miss Foo had relative to the English language were compensated by her medical knowledge, and Mrs. Crawford turned out to be a sweet, compassionate woman who was also a competent administrator. I felt totally ashamed and apologized to them for my childish behavior. In the following months, we became close friends. In fact, they were the first to call me "Doctor." I had to wait a long time for the rest of the hospital to make that acknowledgment.

In Texas a doctor can get his medical license without completing his internship. You merely have to pass an exam. I took the exam, passed, received my license, and began moonlighting in emergency rooms during my free time (which wasn't much). I saved my money for an expensive sports car which I bought after my old banged-up Opel died. (One day the poor thing just literally up and died—stopped dead in the middle of the highway with a loud noise and a cloud of blue-gray smoke from its exhaust. I pronounced it dead at 10:48 A.M. and had it towed to a car dealer. The salesman told me he would pay for the tow truck but could offer me no more as a trade-in. I accepted.)

I told the salesman that I wanted a new sports car with a heater.

"With a heater?"

"Yes, sir. You know, . . . something that heats the interior of the car. My Opel had a heater, but it didn't work, and I never had the money to fix it. So I want to see a new sports car that has a heater."

"Right." He smiled, checking out my battered car and my tattered blue jeans. I could see him thinking, *Got a live one here. A real hayseed.* He turned to the other salesman. "He wants a new car with a heater." Turning again to me, "Well, let me show you our latest model that has a factory-equipped heater built right in. Can you imagine that?"

"They've gone about as fer as they can go, right?"

"Exactly. Not only that but it has air conditioning. Now, in your Opel," he looked at my car and winced, "you may have noticed how hot it gets in these blistering Texas summers. What an air conditioner does is—"

"Can the crap."

"I beg your pardon?"

"I said 'can the crap.' You want to sell a car, and I want to buy one. Let's not go through all this meaningless baloney. I'll take that car there. You fill out your papers, and I'll sign my check, and we'll both be happy, okay?"

He noticed the M.D. on my check. "I'm sorry, Doctor; I thought you were serious about the heater."

"I *was* serious about the heater."

"What kind of a doctor are you?"

"A good one. Pleasure doing business with you."

Thus, armed with a new car and a new M.D., I became socially desirable. Very desirable. I bought new clothes and made sure not to button the top button of my shirt. Gold chains and all, I joined the swinging singles of Dallas. Fast cars and single bars. I was a real hot dog.

Dallas is blessed with some of the most beautiful women in the world. The high-school cheerleader or the drill-team performer graduates from places like Muleshoe, Earth, Dimebox, and Buffalo Gap and migrates to Dallas to seek her future (husband?). If Daddy has money, she enrolls in Southern Methodist University. If Daddy is broke, she works for one of the many insurance or oil companies. In either case, her money is spent on clothes and cosmetics, and she knows how to wear them. And she goes to single bars to dance, drink, and meet men.

The flesh factories on Greenville Avenue catered to these beautiful, well-dressed women. They offered free drinks to unescorted ladies, knowing full well that unescorted ladies drew unescorted men, and the unescorted men would ritualistically buy drinks for the unescorted ladies, and this meant a booming business.

For a short period of time, I was one of their chief patrons. These places were always S.R.O., and I stood, drink in hand, along with the other lonely men seeking lonely women for brief sexual encounters. One-night stands were better than *M.A.S.H.* reruns.

Lonely and phony—that's what we were. All trying to be something we weren't. The men were all single, though the pale circle of evidence on ring fingers testified that many had buried their wedding rings in their pockets; the salesmen were all "regional directors" or "manufacturer's reps"; the store clerks were all "in retail"; the secretaries were all "administrative assistants." I wasn't an intern; I was a budding Jonas Salk or Christian Barnard.

Tired of ending the evenings drunk and alone or drunk and alone with a hooker I had picked up on Cedar Springs Avenue, I decided to postpone my philandering until my work schedule became a little easier. As interns, we were on call every third night, and with my moonlighting jobs, I just didn't have time to drink with all the beautiful people. I wanted to learn medicine.

Baylor University Medical Center was the largest hospital in Dallas and one of the largest private hospitals in the country. I was fortunate to be doing my internship there. For the first several months, I observed. I observed the attending doctors and nurses, but mostly, the residents. They were proud, cocky doctors who could diagnose and handle any type of hospital emergency quickly and with confidence. The chief residents were at the zenith of their medical training. Because they read, studied, taught, and daily applied their knowledge, they were better doctors than the older attending physicians. In acute crisis situations, the older doctors would stand back and watch a chief resident take over and do it successfully. The residents were the hospital's first line of defense. They were good and they knew it.

I stood in awe of these superdoctors. I followed them around and took copious notes (all interns carried a small notebook in their pockets; we called them our "second brain"). I memorized the lab work they ordered on individual cases, asked why they ordered those particular tests, and asked what information they got from those tests. I memorized the treatment for specific diseases. I asked what drugs they used and why and in what dosages. Then I would go home at night and pull out my textbooks to check on various treatment modalities used by the residents. They were always right; in fact, they were doing things that weren't even in the textbooks yet. Often they would cite a specific journal article that had appeared recently. "That's the latest thing," they would announce proudly.

I memorized the sequence of diagnostic tests and therapeutic regimens. "If this test is negative, you can rule out 'X' disease—no sense pursuing that any longer. If that test is positive, then order 'blank' test to confirm your diagnosis. Simple deductive reasoning. If this drug's not working, use 'X' drug. The mode of action is similar, but the slight difference in the pharmacology may be the key. Remember, all patients respond differently, and few patients present the classic textbook symptoms of disease."

I learned that nothing was trivial in medicine. There were no "minor" surgeries, only minor surgeons. . . .

When my resident called me to the emergency room to help him with an "ant bite," I laughed into the telephone. "Are you joking?"

"Get down here stat, Gehring. I need you."

Why does he need me for a simple ant bite? He must be tired and wants me to do the scut work. Unless . . . an allergic reaction? Of course! I started running.

When I arrived the patient, an elderly man, was gasping for air. There were red welts on his body, but his face was blue. He couldn't breathe—bronchospasm.

"Get an i.v. going, Gehring. This man is dying. I've given him antihistamines and epinephrine (Adrenalin), and I can't reverse his bronchospasm. Still think I'm joking?"

I started the i.v. as the resident recited the patient's history. "Seventy-two-year-old white male was playing golf with his son. Complained of stinging sensation on his right ankle. Several minutes later, began wheezing and fell to his knees . . . in an ant hill. His son began brushing ants from his body and rushed him here. On the way the patient complained of tightness in the chest, severe itching, and eventually the gasping that you see now. What's your diagnosis?"

"Anaphylactic shock secondary to insect bite," I replied.

The resident checked the patient. The man's breathing was less labored, the epinephrine was doing its job. "What diagnostic tests would you order to confirm your diagnosis?"

I thought for a moment. Was he trying to trick me? "John, I wouldn't order any tests. Why waste time? The patient presented as an acute medical emergency, and the diagnosis is evident in the history."

"Good, just keeping you on your toes, Bob." The patient was almost breathing normally. "Hi, Mr. Johnson, feeling any better?"

"Much," the patient said hoarsely. "What happened?"

"You had an allergic reaction to the ants that bit you. Have you ever had an allergic reaction before?"

"No, sir, never. And I've had an ant bite before."

The resident made a note in his chart. "Okay, just rest and relax. You're going to be okay." He turned to me. "Okay, Bob, let me continue with the patient's physical examination. The patient presented in acute distress with a blood pressure of eighty-four over fifty and a weak thready pulse. Why?"

"He was in vascular collapse. Because of his severe allergic reaction, the serum in his arteries and veins seeped out into the cellular spaces. There was not enough serum in his vessels to keep his blood pressure up, nor to give him a strong pulse."

The patient was listening intently.

"If his veins were collapsed, how'd you get that i.v. in so easily?"

"Just lucky I guess."

"Glad you didn't say you were good, Bob. Only residents can be that cocky." He smiled. "Okay, why the wheezing and gasping for breath?"

"The edema [serum in cellular spaces] was causing the tissues in his larynx to swell, thus blocking his airway. Untreated, the tissues would have swollen shut, and he would have died of asphyxiation."

Mr. Johnson grimaced, and the resident addressed him. "Mr. Johnson, I want you to hear all this. It will give you an understanding of the severity of your allergy and the necessity of avoiding the antigen—namely ants. I'd suggest you find another golf course." Then he was back to me. "Okay, Bob, you've explained the wheezing and gasping, the low blood pressure, the weak pulse. What about the red welts on the skin and the severe itching?"

I was ready. "Caused by the release of histamine, John. Usually there will be only a local histamine release at the site of the bite. In Mr. Johnson's case, there was a total body release of histamine."

"Good. That's why antihistamines are the treatment of choice, aren't they?"

"Yes, . . . ah . . ." (*Think . . . it may be another trick. Remember the sequence.*) "No, John. Antihistamine comes later . . . as an adjunct to . . . epinephrine."

"In what dosage?"

I felt my face turning red. I didn't know. Mr. Johnson was looking directly at me, and I knew he was thinking that if I'd been his doctor, he'd be dead. "I'm sorry, John, but I don't know the dosage."

John didn't reply. The interminable silence was my

reprimand. (It was most effective; I learned and never forgot the dosage of epinephrine.)

Finally he spoke. "Just one more point, Bob. Mr. Johnson tells us he's never had an allergic reaction before, but he knows he's had an ant bite before. Strange, isn't it? Maybe he's not really allergic to ants. Right?"

"No. That first ant bite only sensitized his body to the ants. He suffered no reaction, but his body was then programmed, fatally, for any subsequent ant bites. That's why you always have patients wait in your office after a shot of penicillin. They may tell you they've had penicillin before and had no allergic reaction. But if their first shot programmed them, the second shot could kill them."

"Good, good." He turned to Mr. Johnson. "I'll come back in a minute and talk to you, sir."

He ushered me into the hall and pulled his patient list from his pocket. "We've got a Mrs. Brown in 3427 in congestive heart failure. I just saw her a short time ago, and she's stable. I know you're tired of congestive heart failures. So am I. It seems we've had a run on them lately on our service. But somebody's got to do it. I'll make you a deal. You get Mrs. Brown toned up and I'll give you a good case."

"How good?"

"A real dandy. Didn't you once tell me you worked in a drug rehab hospital during med school?"

"Yeah, mostly heroin addicts. Why?"

"Know anything about barbiturate addiction?"

"Little bit. Come on, John, tell me. Quit playing games."

He laughed. "We've got an ophthalmologist in intensive care on a respirator, . . . overdose of reds [Seconal]."

"A doctor?"

"Yep."

"Suicide?"

"Nope. At least not intentional as far as we know. Haven't talked to him yet. . . . He came in gorked and is still gorked, . . . but his wife told me he's been eating reds for years. The jerk's addicted. Probably just made a mistake and took too many. In any case, he ain't breathing too well. You want him?"

"You bet I—" Before I could finish, the overhead pager interrupted us.

"Dr. Heart, stat, Room 5425. Dr. Heart, stat, Room 5425." Both John and I instinctively ran for the elevator.

Every hospital has a code for emergencies on the wards. At Baylor, "Dr. Heart, stat" meant that the patient's heart and respiration had stopped. "Stat 13" meant that the patient had stopped breathing but still had temporary heart function. If the patient was terminal, his attending physician would leave a written order, "No Dr. Heart." In other words, let him die.

We were halfway to the 5th floor when John remembered Mr. Johnson. "Oh well, he'll keep. Can't get too far hooked up to an i.v."

I had seen John in a number of Dr. Heart situations before. He was magnificent. Crude, vulgar, obnoxious, short-tempered, but totally magnificent. He took full command of the situation, screaming obscenities at the interns, the nurses, and even the unconscious patient. "Don't die on me, you ____!" They usually didn't.

"The nurses hate me—" he would say, "—even some of the interns. But when they get in trouble, I'm the first one they call, cause they know I'll bail them out. I'll never win a popularity contest, but I sure save lives. I've papered my walls with their petty incident reports. I can recite Sparks's 'Let's talk, Doctor' speech by heart. Now he just mails the things to me. I know I've got an ego problem, but if I were dying, I'd want me for a doctor." I agreed with him on both points—silently.

John literally pried the elevator doors open and raced for 5425. Noise and confusion. The room was packed with nurses and interns. We couldn't even see the patient. John pushed his way through, pounded the patient's chest.

"I want two interns and four of the best nurses to stay.

The rest of you death-loving ghouls get lost. Especially you fat, senile nursing supervisors. I don't want you in my way."

John was intent on inserting a tube in the patient's airway. The nurses were still milling about; they didn't know who should stay or who should leave. He glanced up quickly and saw the confusion.

"Do I have to waste my time making simple decisions for you air-heads? Interns: Ivy and Gehring. Nurses: Sally, Joan, Judy. And where's that Jap that can't speak English. At least she does what I tell her."

"She's Chinese, and she works nights, Doctor."

"Okay, you . . . you draw up some bicarb and get it going. The rest of you, shag out of here!"

John had the endotracheal tube in the patient's windpipe. I attached a bag to it and began breathing for him. John was barking out orders at a volume of 80 decibels above tolerance. You could hear him in the morgue. "Okay, you old goat, I'm going to give you your life back. Just bear with me."

The EKG still showed a flat line, only rising to reflect the compression caused by the other intern's external cardiac massage.

"More bicarb," John shouted.

He was drawing adrenaline into a syringe. "Judy, get the paddles charged. We're going to shock his little heart into beating. Unplug the EKG and stand clear."

The patient's body arched and jerked as the 400 watt-seconds of electricity hit his heart. Shades of Dr. Frankenstein, but it frequently worked. This time it didn't—his EKG still showed activity but no spontaneous beat.

John's face showed concern. Although the patient's heart was not beating, our rhythmic pressure on his chest was forcing some oxygenated blood into his arteries; his brain was getting some oxygen. Not much, but some. But unless we could trigger his heart into action, he would die soon.

"Draw up adrenaline into a cardiac needle. We've got to

put it where it's needed. Gehring, relieve David on the heart massage—he's getting tired. Joan . . ." John was shouting orders in rapid-fire succession. He was worried, but still in control. My kind of general.

He grabbed the cardiac needle from the nurse. The syringe containing the adrenaline tottered on a needle at least three inches long. A formidable weapon. He fingered the patient's chest for familiar landmarks between the ribs— the heart was directly below. Finding his landmarks, he took a deep breath, gritted his teeth, and plunged the needle through the chest wall, terminating the penetration at the desired depth of the heart. (*How does he know?*) He drew back on the plunger and dark maroon blood filled the syringe containing the adrenaline. A perfect shot—he was in the chamber of the heart. He smiled and quickly pushed the blood-adrenaline mixture back into the heart.

"Are the paddles charged?" he shouted.

"Yes, Doctor."

A well-dressed man burst into the room as John reached for the electrical defibrillator. "What are you doing?" It was the patient's attending physician. "I ordered a 'No Dr. Heart' on this man. He's terminal. Let him die in peace!"

John was placing the paddles directly over the heart. He never looked up. "That's just fine, Doctor. I wasn't notified. If you want to kill him, have at it, he's your patient. But you're going to have to kill him after I save him. Stand clear."

The older doctor slammed the door behind him just as the patient's body jerked in response to the electric charge. "Live, you ____, live!" John's eyes flared; his face was flushed. He looked like the movie version of the mad scientist. "Plug that EKG in; I think we did it."

The EKG showed a normal rhythm.

"I'm getting a pulse, Doctor."

"Of course you are. He's living again. Keep pushing the bicarb. We've still got to correct his acidosis."

I looked at John. His face was normal again. He had won.

"Gehring, stay here and keep this man alive. I'll go see the congestive heart failure for you, but you see that sorry drug addict in the ICU. I can't believe a doctor would do that to himself. But don't give him any Seconal—that's what he's addicted to."

"I'm gonna have to, John. You have to withdraw a barbiturate addict slowly. Barbs are not a 'cold turkey' drug. If I stop his Seconal abruptly, he'll start hallucinating and will probably die on us."

"I didn't know that. Thanks. Do what you have to do." (*He admitted he didn't know something? Chalk one up for me!*)

John checked the EKG, then listened to the patient's heart. A broad smile creased his face, and he bent over and whispered something in the patient's ear. Then he stood up and left the room.

I still had a lot of work to do to keep the patient alive. "Did anyone hear what John whispered in the patient's ear?" I asked.

The three nurses John had asked for by name smiled. "It's what he always whispers after a successful resuscitation," Sally said. "He says 'Have a good life, Lazarus.'"

"That's a strange name." I checked the patient's chart. I was puzzled. "His name is David Peterson. Who's Lazarus?"

They smiled at my ignorance. "Lazarus was a biblical character who was dead and—"

"Oh, *that* Lazarus. Of course." (*Stupid!*) "I didn't know John was religious."

At this the three laughed out loud. "He's religious, all right, but his god is different than our God. His god is science, specifically medical science. And himself. He took full credit for saving this patient's life."

"What does he say when he loses one?"

"Nothing. He just kicks doors and curses," Judy replied. "He curses himself unrelentingly for days afterward. Mr. Peterson is not a human being to John; he's a biological unit. John pits his ego against death. I feel sorry for him."

"I don't. He's a good doctor."

"Then I feel sorry for you, too. Excuse me. I've got to talk to Mr. Peterson's family." She left the room.

"What was she all upset about?"

"Doctor, if you don't know, we certainly will never be able to tell you."

I didn't know.

When I got Mr. Peterson stabilized, I went to check on the drug-addicted doctor in ICU. He was still in a coma. After receiving the results of the blood gases I ordered, I adjusted his respirator. Then I glanced at the blood barbiturate level. I couldn't believe it! Must be a lab error. I ordered a repeat barb level. Same reading. He had taken many times more than the lethal dose. I wondered why. John had said it wasn't an attempted suicide, but you'd have to want to die to take that many sleeping pills. It would take days for his body to metabolize and excrete that much barbiturate. He'd be in a coma a long time.

I found his wife in the ICU waiting room. Neiman Marcus all the way. At least three carats on her finger. Classy. Megabucks.

"Mrs. Palmer, I'm Dr. Gehring and I'm the intern—"

"I know." She didn't look up from her magazine. "You're the intern helping the resident who's helping the attending on my husband's case. I've been here before."

"Yes, ma'am. And I need to get a hist—"

"Sure. A history." She continued flipping the pages of the magazine as if she were interested in it. "I've thought of typing and xeroxing a hundred copies of his history so I'd have it ready for his next overdose. I've already told the resident. Why don't you ask him?" More flipping.

"Please, ma'am, I know this is sensitive—"

"Sensitive?" She finally looked at me. "Sensitive! It's tragic. It's disastrous. You don't have a human being in there, you've got a blob of spiritless protoplasm. You're still young enough to use euphemisms. I call it like it is."

I knew she wasn't angry with me. She was angry with that "blob of protoplasm." I was just a convenient sounding board.

"Was it an attempted suicide, ma'am?"

"Of course it was."

"I'm confused. The resident said—"

"I know what the resident said. You don't seem to understand, Doctor. He's been slowly committing suicide for years. Now the pace is quickening. First it's a few pills, sleeping pills. Does he sleep? No. They make him euphoric . . . and loaded. So loaded that he doesn't know how many pills he's taken, so he takes more and more. Until he ends up almost dead. But you always save him, don't you?" She almost sneered. "You miracle workers. You and your wonderful respirators. Why don't you do him a favor and let him die this time. You want a history? Here's your history, Doctor. Chief complaint: Drug addiction. Present illness: Overdose. Past medical history: Drug addiction. Any further questions?"

She knew the format, all right. I knew I'd get nowhere this way; I'd have to try Plan B.

"You've described his problem very succinctly, Mrs. . . ."

(*Use your body language to let her know you're interested in her. Lean forward toward her.*)

"But let's talk about *you*."

(*Put your notebook down.*)

"You're a well-dressed . . ." (*Look directly into her eyes.*) "attractive . . ." (*Gently touch her arm.*) "seemingly intelligent lady. I admire you. A woman of lesser caliber would have left him long ago. How have you put up with this madness?"

(*Beautiful! You've learned the science of medicine, now you're learning the art. Get ready for the best history you've ever taken.*)

She put her magazine on the coffee table and turned toward me. The anger was gone; her voice was soft. She told me everything—the years of frustration, anxiety, fear. . . .

Background: She—a rich Highland Park socialite; debutante, country clubs, big bread. He—West Texas rancher ("I taught him how to eat with a fork."); brilliant, AOA (Alpha Omega Alpha—top ten percent of his medical-school class—the Phi Beta Kappa of medical schools); ambitious, personable. "He married me for my money; I married him for his potential. We were both disappointed."

Marriage: "I wanted the status of being a doctor's wife. Sure, I loved him, but he married medicine, then drugs. I never was his true wife."

Medical practice: "Overachiever, one of the biggest practices in Dallas. It seemed he had to prove his worth, to prove he was better than his West Texas background. But he wasn't. He was an embarrassment. Couldn't play bridge . . . or tennis. Knew nothing about the arts. And those stupid cowboy boots. His friends were all the other pedantic doctors. Shallow, arrogant. All they could talk about was medicine—boring."

Drugs: "I didn't know at first. The kids and I never saw him. I wondered how he could work umpteen hours a day and never be tired. I found some pills in his pocket and naively asked about them. He said they were antibiotics— that he had a sore throat. I found out later they were diet pills. Then he started taking sleeping pills. The pressure of his practice, he would say. I didn't question him. Who'd worry about a doctor getting addicted—I didn't even think about it. The man's a genius—he'd never get hooked on drugs."

She went on to tell me about his deterioration—both physical and mental. The psychiatrists: "at least ten different shrinks"; the neglected medical career: "from the biggest practice in Dallas to zip—would you want him to operate on *your* eyes?"; the ostracism: "at first we all protected him, lied for him. His partners did his surgery for him. Then they booted him out"; the drying-out hospitals: "nut houses"; and finally the overdoses.

Medical license: "When his practice went under and his

partners booted him, he just never reapplied for his license. Are you kidding? They'd never let him practice—thank God."

I reached for her hand in true compassion. "Why did you stay? Why?"

She didn't answer immediately. She looked down at the coffee table and then at the opposite wall. No tears, no hysterics. She softly, slowly spoke to the wall.

"I can remember what he used to be. He was a proud, sincere, compassionate young doctor. A genius. And his hands—those gifted hands. His patients worshiped those hands. Those hands gave them their sight. And I worshiped those hands, too, 'cause when he touched me in bed, I tingled. No other hands made me tingle the way his did. I made fun of his cowboy boots and his West Texas accent. But you know something? I was proud of those boots. He didn't know which fork to use, but he had more pizzazz than any of my socialite friends. He didn't need to dress like the other wimps at the country club, 'cause he knew he had class, and he knew that clothes don't give a man class. Nor accent. Nor bridge, tennis, and operas. He just had it."

She looked directly into my eyes. "As much as I hate him, I love him more. He was the only true man I ever knew. I stayed, young Doctor, because I *love* him."

I started crying—I couldn't help it. I just started crying. I excused myself politely and bolted from the room.

(*You dolt! You fool! Concern? Yes. Compassion? Yes. But not a maudlin show of emotions. Bawling! Be interested in your patients, but show detached interest! You're a doctor. What will she think of you—what will the other people in the waiting room think of you? They were staring, you know. Control your emotions, Doctor!*)

I went to the washroom and washed the tears from my face, then sheepishly returned to the waiting room and sat beside her. "I'm sorry."

"Don't apologize." She cradled my hand in both of hers. "Don't ever lose that, Doctor." I didn't understand. She sensed my consternation and continued. "Don't ever lose that sensitivity. Don't let them take it away from you."

(They didn't take it away from me—I gave it to them freely. Tears had no place in medicine. I cried only once in the next several years, and that was over the death of my puppy. I was becoming what I thought a doctor should be.)

Dr. Palmer came out of his coma, and we weaned him off the respirator. I wrote an order for decreasing dosages of barbiturates—gradually withdrawing him from the drug. The order was countermanded by the attending doctor. "You think I'm going to give him Seconal, when Seconal's the drug that's killing him?" I warned him of the impending hallucinations, convulsions, and eventual death of his patient. He was adamant. I didn't argue—I knew my place. I was only an intern. He was an R.D. (real doctor). I decided to wait.

When I made rounds the following day, Dr. Palmer was picking bugs off his legs. With the bugs came pieces of skin—bleeding pieces of skin. Spiders were attacking him. He was incoherent. I called my resident.

"John, this man is going to convulse soon unless he gets some barbs. His doctor won't listen to me. Will you call him?"

"I will, Bob!" He thought for a moment. "Better yet, Bob, go to the library and get every reference you can on barbiturate withdrawal and tape it to the front of the chart. If Dr. Gofter ignores that, I'll order the barbs myself. If he countermands my order, I'll personally give the man his Seconal. Fair enough?"

When I saw the patient that afternoon, he was lucid. There were no bugs, no spiders. The references I had taped to his chart were also gone.

"He sure is looking better, isn't he?" the nurse beamed. "Thanks to Dr. Gofter."

"Sure is. What happened?"

"Dr. Gofter couldn't explain his strange behavior, so he went to the library and got all the references he could on barbiturate withdrawal. It seems barbs are not a 'cold turkey' drug. The addicts have to be withdrawn slowly."

I thanked the nurse and went to the doctor's lounge for a cup of coffee. Dr. Gofter was sitting at the table with a number of other R.D.'s.

"Our patient sure looks good today, doesn't he, Gehring?"

No admission of error. No thanks. No nothing.

"Yes, sir. Real good." (*Another lesson. Don't make mistakes. If you do, don't admit them. Don't look stupid in front of your underlings. Don't be a human being.*)

(We discharged the ophthalmologist several weeks later. He was drug-free; he was to see his shrink for follow-up care for his addiction. I never saw him again.)

I went to see Mr. Peterson, our cardiac resuscitation. He had a strange story to tell me.

"I was dead, wasn't I, Doctor?"

"No, sir. You were close to death, but obviously, you're very much alive."

"Why did you save me? I know I won't leave this room alive. I've been sent here to die. Why'd you save me?" He wasn't angry, just curious.

"God wasn't through with you yet, Mr. Peterson." (*Nice touch, Gehring.*) I couldn't tell him that he was alive because of an error in communication, that he should have been a "No Dr. Heart."

"I'm glad you did." his voice was hoarse and tired, almost a whisper. "I used to be so afraid of death. But when I was dead—"

"Mr. Peterson, you weren't dead. Your heart just needed a little help and—"

". . . it was a very pleasant experience. Death doesn't frighten me anymore. It's much more pleasant than . . . than being like this." He pointed to the tubes protruding from his aged body. "I long for death again, Doctor."

I knew it could be just senility, but he wasn't talking like a senile old man. He was tired, but I felt he wanted to talk.

"What was it like?"

"It seemed like my soul floated out of my body. I was looking down on myself. I could see and hear everything that went on, especially the loud doctor who was in charge."

My interest peaked. He had been comatose when John and I entered the room, and John had left the room before he regained consciousness. But he described a "loud doctor who was in charge." How'd he know? Could Marie Antoinette see and hear after being decapitated by the guillotine? Yes, her brain still functioned until it depleted its oxygen supply. Not long, but she saw the inside of the basket and heard the voices of her murderers. (*Eeecht! Only a weirdo like you would have a thought like that.*)

I was trying to explain it to myself scientifically, but I was totally engrossed in what he was telling me. I quickly ruled out senility.

"For a while I watched what you were doing to me, and then I entered a long white corridor. I say white, but it was not like any white I've ever seen on earth. It was a brilliant white, but it was very soft—it didn't hurt my eyes. The light seemed to be coming from the end of the corridor. The corridor had no doors, and I seemed to float toward the source of the light. It was very pleasant.

"When I almost got to the end of the corridor, almost to the source of the light, I was abruptly jerked back to the beginning of the corridor."

(*The first electric shock?*)

"Actually, there was no beginning to that long hallway, just an end. I began floating down it again. The light was so pleasant, the sounds so muffled—but they were like music I've never heard. I was at the end of the corridor, and I reached out to touch that beautiful light. Something told me that when I touched that light, I would forever have that soft wonderful feeling I was experiencing. I reached, and again I was jerked—it didn't hurt—but I was jerked back here. To this bed."

(*The successful electric shock?*)

"Please don't think I'm crazy, but I was dead, and death is beautiful."

"I think you're one of the sanest men I know."

"Thank you, Doctor. I want to go back. I'm not afraid anymore. Please, let me go back."

Mr. Peterson's heart stopped again that evening. We didn't attempt resuscitation—we watched him die. We let him touch his white light.

Afterward I told John about the experience Mr. Peterson had related to me and asked if he could explain it. (This was the first time I had heard what would later be described as "after-life experiences.")

"Sure, the man was hallucinating because his brain was deprived of oxygen. Deep sea divers with the 'bends' describe similar euphoria. World War II pilots with malfunctioning oxygen masks experienced giddiness and pleasure. It's merely anoxia."

I wondered.

I was now seven months into my internship and still the intern-on-call. Would I ever become a doctor? To Mrs. Crawford and Miss Foo I was a doctor, but not on my own merit. We were merely friends.

I was doing everything I was told to do. I could handle routine cases if given time to double-check my diagnosis and treatment plan. And as long as I had the backup of the resident or the attending physician.

I knew my initiation into doctordom would only come after I was confronted with a life-and-death situation and handled that emergency alone. I dreaded that eventual day. That was big-time stuff. That's what the R.D.'s did. I would have to sign my name on the patient's chart outlining a successful life-saving procedure. Or I would sign the death certificate. Glory or gloom. I remembered my medical-school diploma: ". . . Doctor of Medicine with all the rights, privileges and honors, as well as the obligations and responsibilities pertaining to that degree." I had flaunted the rights, privileges, and honors; soon I would have to accept the obligation and responsibility. I didn't want to.

1:00 A.M. "Dr. Gehring, Dr. Robert Gehring, stat." The overhead pager startled me. I had never been paged stat before. They always paged my resident stat—never a lowly intern.

I answered the page and called the emergency room. "Are you the intern on call?"

"Yes, what's happening?"

"We've got a man down here in congestive heart failure—bad pulmonary edema. He's not breathing too well. His blood gases are horrible. Hurry!" She hung up before I could answer.

The elevator was too slow—I ran down the stairs. The patient had an expression of panic—he couldn't breathe. The nurses had an expression of disappointment. I sensed they wanted somebody other than Bob Gehring, intern on call.

"Call John!"

"We've called John. He's up in ICU and can't get away."

"Then call the patient's attending, and get him here stat."

"He's here," a nurse said reluctantly.

"Where?" The pause was inappropriate. "Well?"

"He's in the call room, Doctor."

I was getting angry. "Look, I'm going to be honest with you. I need help—and I don't have time for idle banter. Wake him up and get him out here—now!"

"Doctor," an older nurse replied. "He's not asleep. He's drunk."

"He's what?" I couldn't believe it. "How drunk is he?" I was grasping for straws—maybe he could tell me what to do, . . . make decisions, . . . anything.

"He's drunk, Doctor. Believe me, he's drunk."

"Call his partner!"

"He doesn't have a partner."

"Call whoever's covering for him."

"Nobody's covering for him. We've called everybody we could think of. We had to settle for you. You're it."

(*Obligations and responsibilities, and he's drunk. When this is over, I'll report him—you bet I will.*)

The nurses were waiting. I put my stethoscope on the man's chest. His heart was galloping—each short breath gurgled through the water in his lungs. He was drowning in his own body fluids. "Lasix *80* mg i.v. bolus. Digitalis *.5* mg i.v." There was no authority in my voice. In fact, each order sounded like a hesitant whimper. The nurses responded appropriately—they were as sluggish as my orders. "Get a foley in to measure his urine output, and read me his numbers." The nurse slowly read the lab report. She paused between each lab value as if to make sure my inexperienced brain could comprehend. (*Dick . . . and . . . Jane . . . run. See . . . Spot . . . jump.*)

"Read the thing!"

She finished hurriedly. "Doctor, I think you should—"

"Nurse, I think that I should think. I don't have time to clutter my mind with your thoughts. Stop talking, and get that foley in." My fear was expressed as anger.

His blood gases told me that his own futile attempt at breathing was ineffective. He was not getting enough oxygen into his blood to sustain life. His heart was racing to compensate for his low blood oxygen. The digitalis would strengthen his heart, but unless I got more oxygen into his system, his heart would further weaken and then stop. I would have to breathe for him with a respirator. But he was semialert. I couldn't put a tube into his windpipe while he was still awake. He'd fight me. His poor heart couldn't stand any more exertion—it was working as hard as it could.

"Draw up 15 mg of morphine."

"What are you going to do?" the nurse glared at me. "Just what are you going to do with 15 mg of morphine." Her fear was also being expressed as anger.

"You're going to give it i.v. push. All 15 mg of it."

"Like hell I will. That's murder! Fifteen mg of morphine

will kill him. I won't be a party to any of this. That much morphine will wipe out his respiratory center, and he'll stop breathing. He'll die!"

"He's dying anyway!" I shouted. "If I don't do something, he's as good as dead."

"You don't know what you're doing. I wish John were here. I'll draw up your morphine, but you'll have to give it yourself. It's your responsibility, Doctor."

(*Stop. Remember what Sparks told you. Let the nurses work for you. If you fight them, they'll make life miserable for you. They know you're scared—it's written all over your face. Your voice reflects fear. They're scared too. You and your nurses are working against each other. Stop, . . . join forces, . . . fight the common enemy.*)

"I'm sorry." My voice had lost its anger. I looked at each of them. "I'm painfully aware that it's my responsibility! I've never been in this situation before. I'm scared. Unless we knock out his respiratory center and breathe for him, he'll die on us. His own breathing just ain't cuttin' it. Look, I wish John were here, too. He'd know what to do. In fact, I wish anybody were here. But they're not. I ain't much, but I'm all this patient has. And I'm all you nurses have. I need your support . . . and assistance. Help me, . . . please."

The only sound in the room was the patient's labored breathing. I prepared the laryngoscope and the endotracheal tube. After the morphine injection, I wouldn't have much time to get that tube into his windpipe. If I failed . . .

"Your morphine is ready, Doctor." The nurse's voice had lost its anger, too.

"Have you ever tubed a patient before?" she asked.

(*Lie to her. Tell her you have. It will inspire confidence.*)

"No, just on rubber dummies."

"You won't have much time. When that morphine hits his brain, it will also hit his stomach. If he vomits and gets that vomit in his lungs—"

"I know. Thanks."

"I'll help you. I'll give the morphine, you get the scope

and tube in your hands—you won't have time to do both. Get ready."

I looked at my patient. For the first time in my life I would be responsible for life or death.

"Morphine's in, Doctor."

I waited for his breathing to stop. It finally did, and I pried his epiglottis up and away. The light on the laryngoscope illuminated a large orifice, and I quickly rammed the tube through it. I attached a bag to the tube and began pushing air.

"No air in the lungs, Doctor," the nurse was listening intently with her stethoscope. "You must be in the esophagus. The large opening is the esophagus, the vocal cords have a much smaller opening. Try again. Hurry!"

"Please don't barf," I said aloud to my patient. I removed the tube and again pried the epiglottis up. I saw the large opening. I pried harder and the narrow slit of the vocal cords was illuminated. A hard target to hit. I rammed again with the tube—it slipped off the cords into the larger orifice. "Damn." The sweat was dripping from my face onto my patient's. Using the laryngoscope as a lever, I pried as hard as I could. I honestly thought it would come through the opposite wall of his throat. My arm muscle hurt under the sustained pressure, but the cords came into perfect view. Just like the rubber dummy. The tube slipped in easily.

"You're in, Doctor Gehring! He's getting air in his lungs. You did it, Doctor Gehring!"

I attached the tube to the respirator and adjusted the dials. "Call the lab and draw his blood gases. His blood oxygen should be rising appreciably now." I was cocky. "And better hit him with some more Lasix. His urine output ain't worth a damn."

"Doctor Gehring, you look like you could use a cup of coffee. Black?"

"Say that again, please."

"I asked if you would like some coffee," the nurse replied.

"No. No. The 'doctor' thing."

"I said, Doctor Gehring. That's your name, isn't it?"

I glanced up to see John standing in the doorway. He smiled. "So you like that Doctor Gehring stuff, do you?"

I blushed. "I didn't—"

"Don't apologize. You deserve it. I've been watching you. Good job."

In the excitement I had been oblivious to everything.

"How long, John?"

"Since the morphine." He laughed. "Got into the esophagus, huh? Been there a couple of times myself. . . ."

"You no good . . . you watched the whole thing. Why didn't you help me?"

"You didn't need help. Welcome aboard, Doctor Gehring."

I didn't sleep that night. I had never been so happy in all my life. Doctor Gehring.

Oh, the drunk doctor? I didn't report him. We all make mistakes.

John gave me more responsibility. "This is your 'Dr. Heart,' Bob. I handled the last one. I'm tired."

I would charge into the room, pound the patient's chest, and announce, "I want two medical students and four of the best nurses to stay. The rest of you death-loving ghouls get lost." I was a doctor.

My last three months were spent on the obstetrical service where I met a gentle, soft-spoken doctor by the name of Jim Boyd. He was a Christian, involved in a religion I had long since forgotten.

Dallas was full of Christians. This was the Bible belt, and they took their Christianity seriously. They had revivals. And they had bumper stickers. (I remember seeing a pickup truck driven by a man wearing one of those adjustable mesh baseball caps with "Diesel Power" printed on it. His bumper sticker read: "God said it. I believe it. And that settles it." His rear window was filled by a rifle rack supporting three large weapons. I hoped I never had to discuss theology with him!)

But Jim Boyd wasn't one of those "are you saved" Christians. I liked him, and we became friends.

He taught me about obstetrics. Not how to give life— "only God gives life"—but how to bring life into the world. Neither of us knew that someday he would bring a life into the world that was dear to both of us—an adult life—my life.

RESIDENCY

Diet Pills, Darvon, Codeine

After that exacting year of internship, I was tempted to end my formal medical training and enter general practice. Another three years of specialty training also meant delayed gratification. But I knew I would—must—practice OB-Gyn eventually, so I should finish my training while I was young, single, and energetic.

While completing my internship at Baylor, I had been impressed with the excellent OB-Gyn department, the volume of surgery, and the well-trained attending staff. If I continued at Baylor, part of my residency training would be done at Parkland; thus, I would have the best of both worlds—a private hospital and a charity hospital. I applied for and was accepted at Baylor. My internship ended on June 30, 1973. I started my residency the next day.

During medical school and internship, my surgical training had been limited to holding retractors and observing surgical procedures. As a senior medical student, I had been allowed to "close" a simple breast biopsy. I broke the needle, and the fragment was lost in the voluminous fat of the patient's breast. We searched for twenty minutes for that broken needle. The operating-room supervisor was a little piqued, to say the least. She had an emergency scheduled for that operating room. Finally, we got a small metal detector and located the fragment. The resident finished the closure.

127

But as a first-year resident, I was the primary assistant in many surgical procedures. The attending surgeons were usually very tolerant and patient with the residents.

"Gehring, you operate like Mr. Goodwrench." The patient was asleep, the anesthesiologist was reading *The Wall Street Journal,* and I was attempting to sew up the incision in the uterus during a C-section.

I laughed. "I know. The last surgeon told me that I operated like a contestant on the Gong Show. Can I ask you a question?"

"You just did," he replied.

"I know, . . . I noticed you never put your fingers into the holes in the instruments. What are they for?"

"They're for fingers, but good surgeons find that putting your fingers in the holes takes too much time. It's quicker to 'palm' them." He demonstrated. "With practice you can exercise as much control without using the holes as you can by putting your fingers into them. And it's so much faster."

And so I practiced palming surgical instruments. The nurses gave me several worn-out instruments, and during my free time I attempted to withdraw matches from matchbooks without resorting to using the fingerholes. It was difficult.

I also practiced tying knots around the telephone cord, the telephone, and coffee-cup handles. I even tied knots around the steering wheel of my car while waiting for traffic lights to change. (I would frequently wear surgical gloves to simulate actual operating-room conditions. Once a policeman pulled up beside me at a red light and, seeing my surgical gloves, motioned for me to pull over. I explained that no, I hadn't just burglarized a house; I was merely practicing my knots. He laughed and wished me a successful career as a surgeon.)

I started my three-month rotation at Parkland Hospital during the winter of 1974. The chief resident informed us that they were short of help and we would be required to work thirty-six hours on and twenty-four hours off during our

Bob Gehring, 1947 (age 5).

"Grade school days in North Dakota" (age 10).

"When I became an eagle scout (left), I added merit badge after merit badge until my own sash was full" (1955, age 13). Older brother Bill is on the right.

"I ran for and was elected to almost every office our small high school had . . . an all-American boy" (age 17).

Bob with his mother, Elsie Gehring (1955).

"I entered the university on a full-ride scholarship . . . I lost it after the first year because of my drinking."

"General Gehring entered the military as Private Gehring" (second from right, back row).

"I had difficulty convincing the Army of my leadership abilities" (American private, age 21).

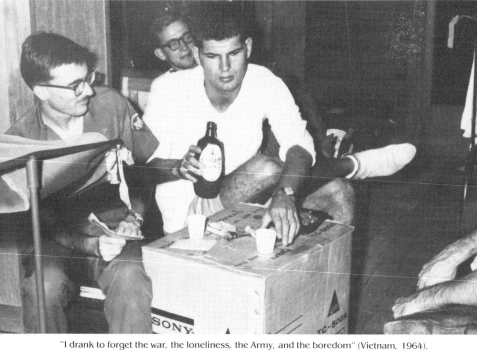

"I drank to forget the war, the loneliness, the Army, and the boredom" (Vietnam, 1964).

"June 5, 1972. Graduation from Southwestern Medical School at Dallas" (with brother Bill).

"I was a medical doctor. I was a somebody."

"I was ecstatic. I had delivered a baby."

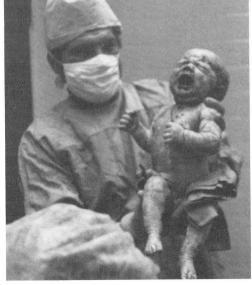

"As I entered private practice, I seriously tried to change my life" (1976).

"But the 'new Bob' was short-lived. And as my practice grew, so did my alcoholism . . ."

"and my drug addiction."

"We spent that Christmas with my parents in North Dakota. . . . It was the last good Christmas we would have for some time." (Bob's parents, Emanuel and Elsie Gehring, knew something was wrong with him but never suspected drug addiction.)

"Carolyn found beauty in everything."

"Carolyn and I were married on May 14, 1977. I took a diet pill, three Darvons, and two sixty-milligram codeine tablets before the ceremony."

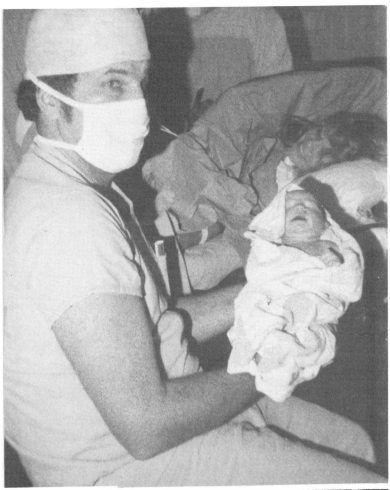

"I held Courtney Robin Gehring in my arms for the first time" (March 7, 1979).

"Happy birthday, little honey. Welcome to our world."

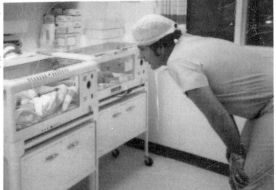

"Dan Griffin and I met every Wednesday
and Saturday."

"Jim Boyd and I met daily for months—he even
called me daily while he was on vacation."

"Telling of his emergence from addiction seemed
to exhilarate Bob, and he began to look for
opportunities to relate his experiences. He proved
to be a spell-binding speaker," said Dan Griffin.
(On television talk show.)

Carolyn and Courtney, 1984.

"As Bob and I grew individually, our marriage became stronger," said Carolyn.

The Gehring family today: Bob and Carolyn, Courtney (age 5), Melissa (age 17), and Gary (age 13).

"Perhaps God did have a plan for my life."

one-month coverage of the emergency room. "It's only for a month—things will be easier for your other two months. During slack times, feel free to get some sleep back in the exam rooms."

There weren't any slack times. Things slowed down around 4:00 A.M., but there was always a patient waiting to be seen. All patients in labor had to be admitted through the emergency room. All pelvic pain and vaginal bleeding were triaged to the OB-Gyn emergency room. The flow of patients was unrelenting.

That year, 1974, was the year of the energy crisis. The world was running out of gas. I would finish my thirty-six-hour shift and fall asleep in gas lines, awakened only by the horn of the car behind me. I fell asleep in the bathtub. (I was too tired to stand in the shower.) Hours later, the freezing water would awaken me, and I'd crawl into bed shivering. I, too, was running out of gas.

Whatever altruism I had was eroded by the fatigue. I was surly and short-tempered. I had little concern for the health of my patients; my only concern was sleep. My patients were definitely short-changed; I was a lousy doctor.

"You in charge here, man?" I had two hours left on my shift. The man across the counter was quite upset, but with a waiting room full of patients, I had no time for public relations.

"Yes, but I don't answer to 'man.' What can I do for—"

"Did you send that nigger in to wait on my wife?" (I had a black medical student on my shift.)

"That 'nigger' is one of the finest young doctors we have in this hospital, and he didn't 'wait on' your wife, he examined her. This isn't a K-Mart."

"Well, let me tell you somethin', Yankee doctor. I can tell by the way you talk you ain't from around here. But down here we don't allow no niggers touchin' white women—get the picture? Or do I have to spell it out for you?"

I was livid, but I knew that any further discussion with this idiot would be fruitless. My job was to deliver medical care, not to educate rednecks on race relations. I thought about telling him to take his wife to another hospital, but then I'd be as bigoted as he. No, I'd examine her.

I walked to the examining rooms. "Tony, did you examine the patient in four?" I asked the medical student.

"She wouldn't let me, Bob. And her husband—"

"I know. What'd you get for a history?"

"Six-months pregnant, abdominal pain, nausea, and some vomiting."

"Probably Braxton-Hicks [false labor pain]. Let's check her for premature labor and get her out of here. Come with me."

We entered the examining room. The patient glared at the black medical student. "I don't want *him* in here when you examine me—no way!"

"That's not your decision, Mrs. Shaw. He stays—and that's that."

"Then I want my husband here."

"Tony, go get her husband."

Tony came back with her husband who was surprisingly silent. Angry, but silent. I listened to the patient's history and did a pelvic exam. She hadn't bathed in days. I explained that false labor pains and nausea were common in pregnancy and wrote a prescription for a drug to control the nausea.

"How about that pain above her belly button on the right?" her husband asked.

"It'll get better." I was tired of these people. I didn't care if it got better or not.

"I want a blood test," her husband pressed.

"Sure, what kind would you like?" (*Anything. Anything at all. Just get it and go. I'm so tired.*)

"You're supposed to know that, man. That's what I'm paying you for," he said sarcastically.

I walked to the door. "Tony, draw a CBC, and let me know the results."

"No, man. I told you I don't want no nigra touching my wife."

I blew up. "Nigra?" I screamed. "Out there he was a nigger. Are you afraid to call him a nigger to his face? You take your smelly white wife, and get out of this emergency room. Do you understand? If you're not gone in thirty seconds, I'll call security and have you removed." I slammed the door behind me.

Several days later, one of the Parkland staff physicians came into the emergency room. "Who's Gehring?" he asked.

"I am."

"Come with me; we need to talk." I followed him to an empty examining room.

"Where's McBurney's point?" he asked.

"It's an area about two inches from the right anterior superior spine of the ilium, on a line between the spine and the umbilicus. . . ." I pointed to my own abdomen.

"What is its significance?"

"It's the point of tenderness in acute appendicitis." I was frightened; I wondered why a busy staff doctor was making a special effort to educate me on appendicitis.

"What about appendicitis in pregnancy?" He was glancing at a patient's chart.

"The point of tenderness moves cephalad with the enlarging uterus. The uterus pushes the appendix higher— the patient may hurt much higher than McBurney's point. Doctor, may I ask the purpose of this impromptu quiz?"

"Do you remember a Mrs. Shaw?"

"No, sir. I see so many patients down here—"

"You sent her home with acute appendicitis."

Silence. My heart was pounding. My mouth went dry. I could feel the blood surge into the capillaries in my face.

"Are you sure it was me?" I don't know why I said that. I knew he wouldn't confront me with such a serious accusation unless he had absolute evidence. I was grabbing for a straw; I wanted the situation to be a perverse April Fool's joke.

"Patient's description of physician: tall, curly hair, Yankee accent. More importantly, your name is on the chart.

You signed her out as 'nausea and vomiting of pregnancy—Braxton-Hicks contractions—not in labor.'" He handed the chart to me.

Shaw. Shaw. My mind labored to match the name with a patient. I studied the chart looking for clues.

"Shaw! I remember her. Those people were garbage. . . ."

"Garbage patients get sick, too, Doctor. Your garbage patient had a hot appendix, and you missed it. You didn't even order any lab on her. . . ."

"Doctor, if I were to order a full lab work-up on all pregnant patients with abdominal pain and vomiting, I'd never get anything done. . . ." (*That's right, make a mistake—get defensive. Try to justify your ignorance.*)

"By that line of reasoning, let's not order EKG's on people with chest pain, right?"

I looked down at the floor. "I'm sorry. I was tired; . . . it's the schedule. . . ."

"Let me paraphrase Winston Churchill. 'Most of the significant contributions to society are made by people who are tired and don't feel well.' Doctors don't get tired enough to miss an appendix. Do I make myself clear?"

"Yes, sir. How is she?"

"Mrs. Shaw underwent an appendectomy at Methodist. She's doing well. I don't know if they'll sue you or not, but they have every reason to do so. Not only did you screw up, but they said you were extremely rude. Ninety percent of lawsuits are caused by bad PR, and your PR was definitely not in your best interests. You've got malpractice insurance, so don't worry about it. But don't let it happen again."

He left me sitting in that empty examining room. He was right. I had forgotten about the equality of medicine. Personalities are not involved when you're dealing with disease. "Garbage patients get sick, too." I had made a colossal mistake.

I wasn't worried about a lawsuit. I was worried about killing someone. A mistake in the practice of medicine was a little more serious than misspelling a word in a spelldown or gluing a wrong piece in a model airplane. I went to see the chief resident.

"I'm making mistakes," I told him.

"I know. I heard about the appendix."

"I'm tired. I can't work thirty-six hours without sleep."

"You can and you will. If you can't cut it, then I'd suggest you go into dermatology or radiology. That's straight eight to five."

"I don't want to be a dermatologist. I don't think you understand. The human body cannot function thirty-six hours straight without screwing up. We're not dealing with dented fenders or leaking faucets. We're talking human lives—"

"I don't think *you* understand, Gehring. I've only got so many residents. Two of them are on vacation. They deserve it. The rest of us have to double up to cover them."

"Us? What's this *us* junk? A chief resident is on call every sixth night. And the nights you are on call, you sleep all night and make us do all the scut work. Did you ever consider helping us out, before someone gets hurt?"

He was angry. "Listen, smart aleck. I've put in my time. I've put in many a thirty-six-hour shift when I was a first-year resident. Rank has its privileges. When you're a chief resident, if you make it that far, you can sleep all night, too."

"That's very comforting, *Doctor.* But it smacks of fraternity hazing, doesn't it? I've been through it, therefore you have to go through it, even if it is detrimental to the patients we're supposedly trying to help. . . ."

His face reddened. "Let's face it, *Doctor,*" he threw back the same sarcastic inflection. "You're just trying to camouflage your own incompetence by using the flimsy excuse of fatigue. I mean, really, . . . missing a classic case of appendicitis. None of the other residents have complained of fatigue—"

"That's hogwash and you know it!" I screamed. "Paul was up here yesterday, and you gave him the same song-

and-dance when he complained about the schedule. You're a liar!"

We both fell silent. I knew I was getting nowhere. I turned and opened the door.

"Gehring?"

I paused. "Yeah?"

"Take speed," he said jokingly.

"What?"

"Never mind."

I closed the door behind me and sat at the nurses' station. I buried my face in my hands.

"Dr. Gehring, the exam rooms are full, and so is the waiting room. Are you going to start seeing patients soon?" The nurses were fresh; they were just starting their eight-hour shift.

"I'll catch up in a minute. I just need some time to think," I replied.

So you're tired. So you screwed up. Learn from your mistakes. . . .

"I am learning. I've learned that doctors can't afford the luxury of making mistakes."

Be logical. Doctors are human beings. Human beings make mistakes. Therefore, doctors make mistakes. Simple, isn't it? Unless . . . of course. You're beginning to believe that Medal of Divinity stuff, aren't you? You think you're a Medical Diety. Do I need to remind you that you're a farm boy from North Dakota who has achieved the degree of Doctor of Medicine—nothing more?

"I know that. But I've worked so hard to get this far, . . . I can't screw up now. I can't let the fatigue get to me."

What are your options? You're not going to quit OB-Gyn. Dermatology ain't your bag, remember. And you've tried to change the system and failed. What's left?

"Diet Pills."

He was joking.

"Was he? I'm sure many residents take a stimulant from

time to time on a short-term basis. My friends in medical school did."

And remember what you thought of them? You thought it was a form of cheating, didn't you?

"But they passed their exams, didn't they? And they didn't get addicted. . . ."

How do you know? And with your history of alcohol and marijuana abuse—

"I AM NOT AN ALCOHOLIC! I am a medical doctor, and I've seen enough drug abuse to serve as an adequate prophylaxis against my own addiction. What's more, I know all the pharmacology of diet pills. I know how they affect every organ system in the body. Doctors are too smart—"

Was the ophthalmologist you saw as an intern too smart?

"As I said, I've seen too much drug addiction to ever become addicted myself. And it's only for the remaining two and one-half weeks of this month. My ultimate objective is to practice OB-Gyn. If that means two and one-half weeks of diet pills, so be it. The end justifies the means—"

"Dr. Gehring," the nurse interrupted my argument with myself, "we're really stacked up. I can't do anything more until you start seeing patients. I know you're tired, but . . ."

I finished that thirty-six-hour shift and drove to my girl friend's apartment.

"Will you pick up a prescription for me?" I asked.

"Sure, need some penicillin? Why don't you just call it in?"

"No, this is for a controlled substance. It has to be a written prescription."

"What's it for?"

"Amphetamines."

"You're not fat."

"I know, but I need something to stay awake."

She started laughing. "You've always lectured me on the evils of diet pills. What a switch!"

"I'm not taking them to get high," I said angrily. "I just need to stay awake."

"Okay, okay. I'm sorry. You've sure been a grouch lately. I wish they'd put you on an easier schedule. I'll pick up your script for you, but I want some of the pills."

"Why?"

"'Cause I'm fat."

"All women think they're fat. Sorry, no pills."

"Then get them yourself."

"Okay, you get two pills. That's all. Deal?"

"Deal."

The following day I started my shift with two capsules in my pocket. After twelve hours I took my first diet pill. I saved the other for the last twelve-hour stretch.

Within fifteen minutes of taking that capsule my energy was limitless. I found that a cup of coffee enhanced that energy level even more. I was no longer intimidated by a full waiting room. My diagnostic acumen was heightened. I had no fear of making mistakes. I was everything I thought a doctor should be.

I finished that emergency-room rotation with the help of the amphetamines. I had calculated the exact number of pills to get me through the month, and when I finished that grueling rotation, I had no desire to continue the pills. I just stopped. No big deal. I didn't take drugs again for months after that. But in the back of my mind, I knew that there was a chemical to keep me alert when I was tired and that I could safely take that chemical without fear of addiction. After all, it made me a better doctor. I made no mistakes.

I returned to Baylor to finish my last two years of residency. The on-call schedule was markedly easier (every fifth or sixth night) so I had more time to moonlight or carouse. Private hospitals were always looking for residents to staff their emergency rooms. I could finish my regular duties at Baylor and work a twelve-hour shift at some ER. Usually, I would get some sleep. If not, there was always a diet pill to get me through the following day.

As a senior resident, I read Pap smears for the attending physicians at Baylor. Reading Pap smears is almost as boring as baseball scores on TV, but I found that diet pills made this task almost palatable.

Hospitals don't pay their residents much, but the supplemental income from my moonlighting tasks proved to be lucrative indeed. And as long as I had diet pills, I could moonlight as much as I wanted. I bought a house. I traded my 240-Z for a Mercedes 450 SL. I took my dates to the most expensive restaurants in Dallas. The pills gave me the ambition and energy to make more money—to have an elegant lifestyle. Better living through chemistry.

The diet pills not only made me a better doctor, but also a better person. Normally reserved, I was now adventuresome. Normally dull, I became witty and clever. Whatever feelings of inadequacy I had were erased by that surge of energy. I could do anything.

I didn't use drugs daily (only addicts were that dependent). In fact, I would go for months at a time without any chemicals (except the ever-present alcohol and marijuana). My drug use was diet pills on a p.r.n. (as needed for) basis. If I *needed* to work all night, I took drugs. If I *needed* to stay awake to drive long distances, I took drugs. If I *needed* to prepare a medical paper, I took drugs.

But soon my p.r.n.'s extended to more mundane efforts: mowing the lawn, washing the car, and balancing my checkbook. I could no longer con myself into thinking I was taking the drugs to stay awake. I was taking them because I loved that euphoric feeling of energy. But I soon found that energy to be dissipated in desultoriness.

Case in point: Saturday morning—a day off. Diet pill at 8:00 A.M. Cup of coffee. Fifteen-minute latent phase, then ENERGY. Objective: Clean and arrange closet. Begin. Stack clothes for dry cleaning. Hmmm. Old telescope I bought at auction sale—let's see if I can fix it. Begin fixing telescope. Need another tool. Tools in garage a mess. Begin rearranging garage. Notice oil leak under car. Begin fixing oil leak.

Car too dirty to work on. Begin washing car. No car polish. Drive to K-Mart. Notice shrubs for back yard. Begin planting shrubs in back yard. Water hose leaks. Begin fixing water hose . . .

It seemed I was always busy, but I never got anything done. I had fifty projects going—none were completed.

Now that I had the time, money, and incentive (amphetamine induced) to spend hours with the beautiful people of the singles' set, it seemed I was vying for the most-eligible-bachelor award. But I never went to a singles' bar without swallowing a pill first. The combination of alcohol and amphetamines made me so intelligent and charming. I had no fear of rejection from the opposite sex. I became aggressive (obnoxious?), and the more aggressive I became, the more successful I was at meeting and wooing attractive women. That M.D. I flaunted was an introduction to all the philandering I could handle.

Where did I get the drugs? Sometimes I wrote prescriptions for girl friends. "I just want to lose a few pounds, you understand." (I had already begun the deceit.) But amphetamines were a schedule-II drug (controlled substances) and I didn't want my name on a bunch of prescriptions for controlled substances. Nonamphetamine diet pills, however, were distributed freely by the pharmaceutical detail men (salesmen). "Doctor, have your patients tried this new anorexic? It's nonamphetamine, but it provides safe and effective weight loss for your obese patients. Do you need some samples?"

"Sure. Send me about a hundred or so." I began eating my mail.

But something was missing. The M.D., the money, and the women were fun, but I was beginning to feel . . . well, . . . guilty about the lifestyle I was leading. Especially about the drugs. I began having periods of depression and terrible, unrelenting headaches. I was lonely, and I was worried about getting too dependent on the pills.

Balderdash! You can stop anytime you want to stop.

You're strong! Just wait until you get into private practice. We're talking big money and status then, friend. Hang in there. I've taken care of you so far, haven't I?

"Well, I suppose."

Sure I have. The guilt, depression, and headaches are all throwbacks to that outdated morality you heard about in Sunday School. Come on, let's go to the elixir department again, and I'll fix you up.

"More drugs, huh?"

Nothing you need to worry about. You've prescribed Darvon or codeine for many of your patients with headaches because you know they're only mild analgesics. Their addiction potential is very low—you know that. And they'll help with the depression, too.

"You promise I won't get addicted to them. I'm kind of concerned—"

Not a chance. Trust me.

I was a modern-day Faust.

On April 5, 1976, Howard Hughes died on a flight from Mexico to Houston. As I read the account of his death in the newspaper, I wondered if his drug addiction contributed to his death. I was sure it had. I felt sorry for him. A loner. Billions of dollars and still alone, watching *Ice Station Zebra* in a blacked-out hotel room. Sad.

I, too, was alone. I had stopped going to pick-up bars months before. I could call any number in my black book and have immediate company and sex, but I didn't want to. My Mercedes had lost its appeal. My better living through chemistry had deteriorated into a Howard Hughes existence. I needed a drug to get out of bed in the morning, alcohol to go to sleep, marijuana to have sex, and Darvon or codeine for my headaches. My depression deepened.

I bought a house on a lake close to Dallas. Spent thousands of dollars on expensive furnishings. Bought a whole new wardrobe. I still wasn't happy.

I sat for hours, crying, in my beautiful new house. I

didn't answer the phone. I ignored my old friends and refused to make new ones. I just sat.

I reflected on the reasons for my depression. It seemed I was never happy in the present—the here and now. I wanted to go back to the farm. Life was so simple there. No big-city pressures, no traffic, no rat race. But I knew the pressures my father had as a farmer. The low price of wheat—the high price of machinery. Crop failures. Hailstorms that could wipe out a year's income in seconds. And I wasn't a farmer.

I lived in the future. I'll be happy when: I get out of the Army; I finish college; I finish med school, internship, residency. I'll be happy in private practice; I'll be happy when I get married; when I have children. I was never happy in the only moment of time over which I had any control—the present.

The only thoughts I had during that severe depression were: I am no good; life is not worth living.

Drugs were the only relief from this torment, but I was even building a tolerance to them. My usual maintenance dose was not enough, and I had to study for my board examinations. I couldn't concentrate in that bottomless pit of despair. If one diet pill didn't energize me, I took two. If one Darvon didn't work, I took two, . . . three, . . . or four at a time. The end justified the means; I needed to pass that exam.

I don't know how I passed. The drugs made me a raving maniac. I tried to camouflage my lunacy in front of my colleagues. "It's the stress of the test, nothing more." But my close friends saw a definite personality change.

After finishing the test, I returned home and vomited. My drug-wracked body could not tolerate any more chemical abuse. I flushed the remaining drugs down the toilet and sat weeping in my empty house. I swore I would never take a pill again.

PRIVATE PRACTICE

Darvon, Codeine, Demerol

On that terrifying night after my board exams, I had called one of my girl friends, Carolyn Boswell, and begged her to spend the evening with me. "Something is going on in my life that I can never tell you about—something very bad." I didn't tell her what the "something" was, but she came.

Carolyn was not like the other girls I had dated. She was honest and sincere and disarmed me with her naive frivolity. And she liked me. I needed someone to like me, because I certainly didn't.

My initial attraction to Carolyn had been pure lust. Another resident had told me to "check out" the beautiful, sexy woman sitting in the waiting room. Wow! I made a clumsy attempt to introduce myself, then assisted in the Cesarean delivery of her nephew. I pestered Carolyn's sister (poor woman—she had just undergone major surgery) until she gave me the pertinent information. Was she married— no. Did she have a boyfriend—of course. What was her phone number—ask her. Finally she relented, and I hastily scribbled the number on my scrub-suit pants.

Carolyn was a lady, and I wasn't accustomed to ladies. The women I had loved had all abandoned me—my high-school sweetheart, my college girl, my ex-wife. For years I purposely avoided any form of lasting relationship—the pain of rejection was too intense, and I didn't want that pain to interfere with my medical education. So my "relation-ships" were with bar girls and hookers. They were no threat to my self-imposed isolation and certainly didn't impede my status-seeking efforts.

Carolyn was different. She was a divorcee with two small children, struggling to make ends meet in the rat race of Dallas's oil industry, yet she never complained. She was determined to give her children a happy home life filled with courtesy, love, and respect. She was an excellent mother (and father), and that impressed me.

But it was her childlike enthusiasm for life that captivated me. Once, early in our friendship, when Dallas was blessed with an infrequent snowstorm, I found her sitting on the edge of her chair in front of the window with her two children gathered close to her. She was clapping her hands in gleeful appreciation. "Look at the size of those snowflakes. Isn't it beautiful?" The kids were excited, but not nearly as much as their mom.

She found beauty in everything—even me. She saw through my big-doctor-bravado and discovered the lonely, frightened little boy that I tried so hard to conceal. And she accepted and understood me as I really was.

She also had a faith in God that I envied. I smiled whenever I heard her little "one-liners" to the Almighty. "Dear God, don't let my hair go straight today," or "Dear God, don't let me be late for work," or "Dear God, don't let the cookies burn."

As I entered private practice, I seriously tried to change my life. I joined an established partnership of three OB-Gyn doctors. They and their office staff were friendly, likable people who went out of their way to make me feel welcome. I stopped introducing myself as *Doctor* Gehring—I was just plain Bob. I spent more time with Carolyn; I renewed old friendships. I started playing golf (don't all doctors?), and I stopped taking drugs (except for alcohol and marijuana, of course).

Incongruously, my income suffered a drastic reduction

when I entered private practice. I had to stop moonlighting in emergency rooms because I couldn't be tied up if a patient of mine went into labor. Initially, of course, that was unlikely because I had few patients. I spent most of my time talking to the office staff or reading in my office. "Dr. Kersee can't see you for three weeks, but we have a new doctor who will be glad to see you."

"When?"

"Anytime you want."

If a patient finally did show up, I talked to her for hours. Frequently they would interrupt me and say, "Doctor, I enjoy chatting with you, but I really must get back to work." Soon I had the reputation of being a doctor who would spend time with his patients and answer their questions. My practice grew.

But the "new Bob" was short-lived. As my practice grew, so did my lust for status. It wasn't the money. I wanted a big practice because a big practice reflected my ability as a doctor. I needed that ego trip. And as my practice grew I found that I needed stimulants to work the long hours. Yet I felt guilty about the money I was making. I knew that the money I made was tainted. It was drug money.

I remember thinking to myself, "Is this all there is?" I had come from a wheat farm in North Dakota and was now a big-city doctor at one of the finest hospitals in the country. I had money, lots of money. I had sex. I had *status*. All the things I'd ever wanted. Why wasn't I happy?

Look to the future again, I decided. When I got married, I'd be happy. I had found "my person"; I was in love with Carolyn. Why wait any longer? Marriage would solve all my problems.

Carolyn and I were married on May 14, 1977. I took a diet pill, three Darvons, and two sixty-milligram codeine tablets before the ceremony.

We postponed our honeymoon until after the celebration of my parent's fiftieth wedding anniversary for which we drove to North Dakota. (I needed the amphetamines again. Couldn't risk getting sleepy on the road.) I was so proud to introduce Carolyn to my family. She would "make" me well, and we would live happily ever after.

When we returned from our trip to Europe, however, the honeymoon was over in more ways than one. I was now a married man with two stepchildren, ten-year-old Melissa and five-year-old Gary. They were good children, well-mannered and considerate. But they were children, and children made me nervous. I could only relate to them with the help of alcohol and codeine. Soon even the chemicals didn't ease the tension between us. I retreated to my bedroom and to my drugs. I felt sorry for the kids—I was a lousy stepfather. The kids were scared of me, my wife was scared of me, and I was even scared of myself. I was so terribly angry. (Later Carolyn showed me a diary she kept during those early years. "Bob's depressed again," . . . "Bob's happy," . . . "Bob's mad," . . . "Bob's loving," . . . "Bob's up," . . . "Bob's down." I was a veritable Yo-Yo!)

I was blaming everybody and everything for my unhappiness. The pressure of my job, the marriage, the children.

The friendly doctor who had lots of time to chat with his patients now developed a "hit-em-up—move-em-out" office practice. In order to see the increasing volume of patients, I had to keep the examining rooms constantly occupied, thus shortening the time I could spend with each patient. But I found that patients liked their doctor to be busy. A busy doctor is a good doctor—that's why he's busy. Patients wanted *their* doctor to drive a Mercedes and live in a big house. They envied and perhaps resented the wealth of the medical community as a whole, but *their* doctor should have the best. After all, "he's *my* doctor."

I had good rapport with most of my patients. Some even became close friends. But I couldn't relate to the women who wanted to be sick.

"There's nothing wrong with you, Mrs. Jones."

"But why do I hurt, Doctor?"

"I don't know."

"Are you saying it's all in my head. All you doctors camouflage your ignorance by that statement. . . ."

"No, Mrs. Jones. What you perceive as pain is indeed pain, whether or not there is an organic cause for that pain. I'm merely saying that your symptoms do not fit into any disease pattern or syndrome. Your lab tests are all normal. I can find nothing wrong with you."

"Can you give me something for the pain?"

"Yes, I can give you some pain pills . . . but only on a short-term basis. If you're still hurting, I'll refer you to another competent doctor."

I wasn't a Dr. Feel-Good. My patients knew better than to ask for tranquilizers, diet pills, Quaaludes, sleeping pills, or strong narcotics. "Doctor Gehring doesn't believe in those kinds of drugs—they treat the symptoms, but not the problem," the nurses would tell the patients. "Don't even bother to ask." Who would suspect a doctor of abusing drugs if he had that kind of reputation?

I finally stopped taking diet pills altogether. I was experiencing all the bad side effects—nervousness, irritability, palpitation, insomnia, and impotence. (Carolyn's diary contained many entries of "Bob can't, what am I doing wrong?" She was blaming herself for my drug-induced impotence.)

Also, I had begun to notice something disquieting about my behavior: whenever I talked to someone—friend, patient, colleague—I would avoid eye contact, directing my eyes down or away as though trying to hide something. It happened so gradually that I can't recall when I first caught myself doing it. But once I realized it, I noticed it occurring with more frequency. I knew the next step would be to avoid personal contact. I was becoming a loner.

And the diet pills were too hard to get. The detail men would leave some samples from time to time, but frequently the demand outstripped the supply. I'd then write a prescription for my mother-in-law, sister-in-law, or other family member.

Writing "scripts" for drugs to family members without their knowledge, then paying for and using the drugs myself was not only unethical—it was illegal. Each prescription was a felony in the state of Texas. But I knew I wouldn't get caught. I'd often know the pharmacist, and we'd chat and joke while he filled the order.

"Granny's on a diet again, huh, Dr. Gehring?"

"Sure is, Jim," I'd reply. "Either that or she's a speed freak." Yuk-yuk. I had become a real con artist.

When I stopped the diet pills, however, I increased the dosage of Darvon and codeine. The samples were plentiful, and I could always order them from pharmaceutical supply houses. Once I received a shipment of two thousand Tylenol No. 3's (acetaminophen and codeine) and stored these pills in the trunk of my car. Carolyn asked what they were, and I told her they were antibiotics for the office. She didn't ask why they were in my trunk, but I quickly found a better place to hide them.

I would take drugs daily for three or four weeks at a time. The Darvon and codeine didn't make me feel sleepy or drugged. In fact, they gave me energy and put me in such a good mood that I was enthusiastic about work, family, and leisure. During office hours I would take just enough to make me energetic. I was in control. There was no staggering, no slurring of speech. I was just a busy, energetic young doctor.

Did the drugs influence my medical judgment? Sure they did, but not to a marked degree at that time. I still practiced good medicine; my thought patterns were still sound. Only later, when the drugs dominated my every waking minute, was I impaired. Even in moderate dosages, however, the drugs tricked me into thinking I was more acutely aware, more on top of a situation than I was.

After a steady drug diet for three or four weeks, I would feel guilty. Then for three or four months I would take nothing. Lethargic and depressed, I'd want to tell Carolyn why I was feeling so rotten. So I'd tiptoe around it, playing games with her and, ironically, with myself.

"Carolyn, there is a reason why I'm feeling and acting this way, but I can't tell you what it is. But please trust me, I'll work it out."

"Is it cancer? Are you dying of cancer?"

I laughed, assuring her it wasn't fatal, and jokingly said, "I'm a mass murderer."

"Oh, thank God. I thought it was something serious," she replied.

Debi Wyatt's near death in 1978 frightened me, but my response to that crisis scared me even more. I actually stuck a needle in my body—a syringe of Demerol. Needles were synonymous with drug addiction. Whatever vestige of denial remained was obliterated by that single act. I knew I was sick.

I called a psychiatrist for an appointment, but I had to cancel because of a delivery. I never rescheduled the appointment. Probably because I had seen psychiatry in action and wasn't impressed. But where does a doctor go when he has a problem? The clergy? My problem wasn't spiritual. And to admit my drug problem to anyone else was out of the question. What if my colleagues found out? My patients? My friends? And I certainly couldn't tell Carolyn and blow my strong-man image. No, I'd have to handle the "problem" myself.

By this time Carolyn was pregnant, and I decided we should celebrate by taking a Mediterranean cruise. We could afford it. The oldest doctor in our group had stopped doing obstetrics and referred most of his OB patients to me, so that I now had a large, lucrative practice. The money was rolling in.

The week before we were to leave, Carolyn's father, who had been in intensive care for several weeks, died. Naturally,

Carolyn was not in the best of spirits, but her family urged us to go ahead with the trip we had planned.

Carolyn tried very hard to hold back her grief during the trip, but more than once I caught her staring out the window with tears running down her cheeks. A couple of days into the cruise, we had a terrible argument, and I said many things to hurt her. Ugly things. It seemed I wasn't satisfied until I said something hateful enough to cause her to cry. Only then would I stop my verbal barrage.

Later I apologized. "I don't know what got into me," I said. (I had used those exact words the week before to her sister Glenda, when I blew up at her in the intensive-care waiting room. Glenda had made a few innocuous remarks that I perceived as a personal affront. I had unleashed a tirade of vituperation that brought her to tears, also.)

But I knew what got into me. Drugs got into me. Drugs were always getting into me. Each effort to quit ended in failure, and each failure brought on a despondency that was only relieved by more drugs. A vicious, lethal cycle.

Our ship docked in Haifa, Israel, and we took a bus to Jerusalem. There, we stood on the Mount of Olives and viewed the Holy City across the Kidron Valley. Below us was the Garden of Gethsemane. In the distance was the Wailing Wall of the temple. I remembered these familiar names from Sunday School, but I viewed the landmarks merely from a historical perspective. Carolyn was saying things like, "Can you believe it? This is where Christ actually lived and breathed." But I felt no spiritual impact.

In fact, I felt guilty again. Guilty for having treated Carolyn so shabbily. Her father had just died, and she was pregnant with my baby! I was despicable. I also felt guilty that my Christian parents weren't on this cruise instead of me. To them it would have been a trip of a lifetime, a pilgrimage, a reward for the good lives they had led. To walk the Via Dolorosa would have been the high point of their Christian lives. The high point of my life was swallowing a handful of Darvon.

In the city of Jerusalem we stopped at the Wailing Wall. Orthodox Jews wearing phylacteries were rocking back and forth, the air echoing with the cacophony of their chants. Some even wrote their prayers on paper and placed them between the stones of the wall.

Carolyn entered the roped-off women's section of the wall. I attempted to enter the men's side, but was reprimanded by an angry Jew screaming at me in a strange language. He kept pointing to the top of his head. I returned to the entrance, donned a skullcap, and walked to the faded gray masonry. I put both my hands against the cold stone blocks and closed my eyes. "God, cure my drug addiction." I only said it once; I saw no reason to repeat it. If there was a God, He knew I was a junkie. But I figured it was worth a try; it was worth at least a simple prayer.

We returned to the ship, and I secretly swallowed more pills. Well, there was my answer. He wanted me to be a pillhead. I prayed and He failed me. Didn't He give same-day service?

"What did you pray for at the Wailing Wall?" Carolyn asked.

"Oh, you know. Health and prosperity. The usual prayer things. How 'bout you?"

"I prayed for my children and this baby I'm carrying. But mostly, I prayed for you, Bob. And I firmly believe that God will answer my prayers."

I envied her faith in God. I hoped it was enough for both of us.

I finally kept an appointment with the psychiatrist. I thought I was crazy. Not schizophrenic crazy—I wasn't hearing voices. But I couldn't believe a sane man could be so miserable.

"I think I'm a drug addict," I said.

"Tell me about it." He wasn't shocked. I figured he probably practiced that blasé expression the way I had practiced tying knots.

"Well, it started with diet pills years ago, . . . well, actually with marijuana; . . . to be truthful, it started with alcohol when I was in high school. . . .

He was a good shrink. He encouraged me with well-timed go-with-that's and how-did-you-feel-about-that's, and my favorite, the take-the-last-word-of-his-sentence-and-make-it-a-question ploy. "In high school?"

"Yes, in high school." I told him about my addiction. I omitted the post—Debi Wyatt—demerol incident. I just couldn't tell him that I had used a needle. But I told him everything else.

"How do they make you feel?" he asked.

"At first they gave me energy. Not only the diet pills, but the Darvon and codeine, too. They put me in such a good mood that I felt energetic. Now I take them to feel normal; . . . if I don't take them, I'm too depressed to function. I'm immobilized."

"How much are you taking?"

"About six Darvons and four Tylenol No. 4s."

"A day?"

"Every three hours."

"You're kidding!" His blasé countenance was shattered. "How can you function?"

"Do I look stoned?"

"No."

"It's tolerance. I just took my usual dosage a half hour ago. I've built up to this dosage over a period of time."

"I'm sorry. I understand tolerance to drugs. Please continue."

I told him about the guilt which led to anger, which led to depression, which led to drugs, which led to more guilt. It was a purging, a catharsis, to finally tell another human being of my odious affliction. But before my purgation, I confirmed the confidentiality of the doctor-patient relationship.

"I don't want you to tell anybody," I said.

"I beg your pardon?"

"If I'm going to tell you about my drug addiction, if I'm going to figuratively undress in front of you, I want to know that you won't tell anyone . . . ever."

"First, we haven't established that you are indeed a drug addict. Second, I'm offended. Of course I'll protect your confidence. And third, I sense you have a low opinion of me and the psychiatric profession in general."

"Not you, Doctor. My first impression is that you're a competent doctor. But you're right about my opinion of the psychiatric profession."

"Why?"

"I have a feeling that you shrinks watch a burning house and argue amongst yourselves about where the fire started. You talk about mothers and childhood and anger-turned-inward, and all the while the house is being destroyed by the flames. But as you look at the ashes, you can say 'Aha! The fire started in the basement.'"

"Is your house on fire?"

"That's a typical psychiatric response, Doctor. Yes, my house is burning, and no matter how hard I try, I can't put out the fire. . . ."

He listened to my story and agreed that I was abusing drugs. "But you're not a drug addict."

"I'm not?"

"No, you're severely depressed, and you're treating your depression with the wrong medications. And you're medicating yourself. Remember, 'A physician who treats himself has a fool for a patient!'"

"You're putting me on more medications?" I asked.

"I'm putting you on *different* medications—an antidepressant and a tranquilizer. . . ."

"Didn't Freud make the mistake of proposing cocaine as a cure for alcoholism?"

"There you go again," he replied angrily. "I'm not Freud, and I'm not proposing cocaine. If you want me to help, please *let* me help!"

I stopped taking the Darvon and codeine and began

taking Elavil 75 mg q. h.s. (at bedtime) and Tranxene (similar to Valium) 7.5 mg t.i.d. p.r.n. (three times daily as needed for) anxiety. That's what the doctor ordered, and for several days I followed his prescription to the letter. Then I started taking the tranquilizer four times daily, then five times daily, then two capsules at a time, then three capsules. . . .

"I'm abusing the Tranxene," I told the psychiatrist several weeks later.

"How much?"

"I don't even count anymore. The number just makes me feel more guilty."

"I can't believe you can function. Tranxene should make you sleepy. Doesn't anyone suspect? Your wife? Your colleagues?"

"I'm trying to tell you that I react differently to drugs. The tranquilizers don't make me sleepy. They don't make me feel good, and they don't make me feel bad. They just make me feel . . . different."

"Why do you want to feel different? Do you hate yourself so much? . . ."

"I know, you're going to tell me that I've got everything going for me. That I should count my blessings—"

"You're an angry, bitter man."

"I know that, too. I know all that! I don't want to be a junkie!" I started crying. "I don't want to be an angry, bitter man. I want to be normal. I came to you for help. I've never asked another human being for help before. I'm asking you. Help me!"

He sat there, not saying a word. I had begged him for help, and he just sat there. I didn't expect him to wave a magic wand or pull a rabbit out of a hat, but I did expect something . . . anything.

I knew silence was a psychiatric ploy to get the patient talking. But our time was limited, so I'd play his game.

"I worked in a drug unit in California when I was in medical school," I said softly. "Our success rate with drug addicts wasn't very good. In fact, it was zilch. Has anything changed in the past ten years? Is there a way out of this mess? What's my prognosis?"

"Prognosis? I'm going to be absolutely truthful with you, Bob. Most drug addicts die of their disease, . . . and at an early age. They either commit suicide or overdose accidentally or die in a car accident. They destroy their lungs, kidneys, heart, and especially their liver. They're miserable.

"But many of them are sociopaths—the jails are full of drug-addicted sociopaths. They have no sense of right and wrong. You're different; you have a conscience. You're not taking drugs to get high, you're taking drugs to treat what I call 'chronic psychic pain.' "

"What's that?"

"What you've been experiencing the last several years and what you've been medicating with your choice of drugs."

"The sadness, the depression?"

"Exactly. You may need to be on a maintenance dose of something for the rest of your life. But I doubt if you could stay on a maintenance schedule. Given an opportunity, you'd abuse the drugs."

"Why?"

"If I knew the answer to that question, I'd win the Nobel Prize. Why does the alcoholic drink? I don't know why. But in answer to your original question, the prognosis for drug addiction is slim to none."

There was a long silence. I knew what he was saying was true. I guess I had wanted him to lie to me.

This time he broke the silence. "I have seen some people recover, but in your case, your intelligence may be your biggest impediment."

"Nonsense!" I said eagerly. "How do they recover? Tell me."

"The people I've seen recover have had a religious conversion. They have an almost childlike faith in the power of God. . . ." He saw me slump in my chair. "You look disappointed," he said.

"A religious conversion?"

"Yes, they experience—"

"A Charles Colson, Tex Watson born-again thing?"

"Yes, . . . who's Tex Watson?"

"One of the Manson murderers. You mean I've got to become a Bible thumpin' Jesus freak?"

"Jesus freak connotes extremism. Let's say 'spiritual.'"

"You're talking like the people in Alcoholics Anonymous. They've got this 'spiritual' thing. This 'Higher Power.' I only went once. I was looking for a way out of my addiction, but all I heard was *God, as I understand Him*. I doubt if they really believed in . . ."

"Were they sober?"

"Well, . . . yes, . . . I guess so—"

"Perhaps they were trying to tell you something. But, as I said, maybe you're too smart to get well. We're out of time—see you next week."

I never returned. I knew enough about psychiatry to know he was a good psychiatrist. And I knew he wasn't proselytizing when he talked about the God stuff. It was just a clinical observation on his part: People who got well, had God. Those who didn't, didn't.

But I was a pseudoscientist, and God-talk was the end of the line. In the movies, the Marcus Welby–type surgeon told the concerned loved ones, "We've done all we can, now he's in God's hands," and the patient always recovered. In real life that type of advice would be translated: You can kiss him good-by, he's as good as dead.

Marcus Welby was fine for the movies. But for a "real life" doctor to tell me that the only way to stop was through God was defeatist. It was tantamount to faith healing. I could derive the same therapeutic effect by placing both hands on the TV and having Oral Roberts scream "BE HEALED!" And it wouldn't cost eighty dollars an hour.

I knew, of course, that if I wanted to stop taking drugs, I

had to stop taking drugs. Simple as that. But I wanted something even easier. I wanted medical science to have a cure for my addiction that didn't involve changing my life. I wanted a pill to cure my compulsion for pills.

Before giving up on the psychiatric profession, I sought a second opinion. My new shrink thought I was manic-depressive and started me on lithium.

"Where's the mania?" I asked him. "If I'm manic-depressive, why have I never been manic? At least I could enjoy the euphoria of my mania instead of this gut-wrenching depression."

"It's worth a try," he said. "It's better than the drugs you're addicted to."

After several weeks we both agreed: I wasn't a manic-depressive. I stopped the lithium; in fact, I stopped all drugs, alcohol included.

By now, Carolyn knew I was seeing a psychiatrist. She thought it was for my depression. I'm sure that made sense to her, for she watched me sit for hours in our darkened bedroom and stare at the wall—just stare. I didn't eat; I couldn't sleep. I'd wake up early and tell her I wished the new day had never come.

November 18, 1978. A drug-crazed madman named Jim Jones convinced 912 of his followers to join him "on the other side." As I viewed pictures of their swollen bodies, I began thinking of my own demise. Not only thinking, but planning suicide. Life without drugs was unbearable.

Thanksgiving Day, 1978. I was too depressed to spend the day with Carolyn's mother and her sisters' families, even though I knew how important happy holiday occasions were to the members of her family. She told them I was at the hospital with a patient in labor. (She later told me, "This was the first of many excuses I made for you. At first people believed me. Busy doctor and all. Later they knew I was covering for you. I was a classic enabler.") When she and the children returned, she brought me a plate with turkey and all the trimmings. She found me in the same spot in which she had left me—sitting in my bedroom chair. I had my life-insurance policies in my lap. She didn't realize it, but I had been reading the suicide clauses and had just determined that the two-year waiting period had elapsed. I could kill myself, and Carolyn would still receive the insurance.

Finally, I knew I could no longer conceal the truth from her. So one day, when she had accompanied me to the psychiatrist's office, I had the doctor go out to the waiting room and get her. He told her I had something to tell her. When she entered the room, I couldn't look at her, but sat with my face buried in my hands, sobbing uncontrollably.

"Carolyn, I'm a drug addict," I finally blurted out. "I've been a drug addict for years. I was taking drugs when I married you. I should have told you then. Please forgive me."

Her initial reaction was, "Is that it? Is that all? Is drug addiction your big dark secret? I had imagined so many things that were much more terrible. So what if you've taken a few too many pills?"

Driving home later, she tried to encourage me (she was always trying to cheer me up). "Bob, if you feel so guilty about taking those drugs, just don't take them anymore." Oh, if it were only that simple, I thought, and began to cry again. Carolyn had a lot to learn about drug addiction—so did I.

We spent that Christmas with my parents in North Dakota. Whether it was the novelty of a white Christmas, the excitement of my parents and myself over Carolyn's pregnancy, the absence of drugs, or a combination of them all, it was a good Christmas. I was able to relax more than I had for some time. It was the last good Christmas we would have for some time.

Shortly after the new year, January, 1979, we returned to Dallas, and I began studying for my oral board examination in Obstetrics and Gynecology. I was remarkably cheerful, considering the amount of stress I was under. Too cheerful. I had started taking drugs again.

OUT OF CONTROL

Darvon, Codeine, Percodan, Fiorinal, Methadone,
Demerol, Morphine

"Tell us about patient number thirty-six on your list, Doctor," the good doctor said.

I flipped the pages to find patient thirty-six. "Mrs. McClain was a forty-four-year-old white female—"

"We can read, Doctor," the bad doctor interrupted. "Tell us about your diagnosis."

Oral board examination. The final hurdle to cross to become a Board Certified Obstetrician-Gynecologist. I was forewarned about the proceedings by friends who had taken the test the year before. "You will be quizzed by three doctors: the good, the bad, and the indifferent. The good doctor and the indifferent doctor don't say too much. The bad doctor does most of the questioning, and he can be a real jerk," my friends warned. "It's a sadistic game of one-upmanship. He loves to tear you apart—the more defensive you are, the better he likes it."

I was ready for them. I had passed the written exam, so I was confident of my knowledge of OB-Gyn. I had fortified myself with my usual dose of Darvon and codeine—just to "take the edge off"—and I had a pocketful of pills in case I needed a "booster" during coffee break. Achieving this certification had been my goal for years. I needed those pills—I couldn't quit until after board exams.

"The diagnosis was adenomyosis." I tried to hide the contempt in my voice. The bad doctor had been riding me all morning about my diagnostic abilities. A real wise guy. Some medical-school research wizard. What did he know about diagnosis—the closest he ever came to patients was laboratory rats.

"That was the pathologist's diagnosis, Doctor. Your preop diagnosis was uterine fibroids. The pathologist didn't find any fibroids. What kind of preoperative work-up did you do with this patient?"

"Well, sometimes I get a sonogram, sometimes an IVP, sometimes a—"

"I'm not talking about sometimes, Doctor. I'm asking you about this particular patient."

"My diagnosis with this patient was based on a pelvic examination . . . as much as I remember, . . . but I can't be certain." (*Why can't I remember? He's going to beat me to death on this one. I wish we'd take a coffee break. I need those pills.*)

"Fibroids are pretty easy to feel on pelvic examination, are they not, Doctor?"

"Well, yes, . . . ah, no, . . . well, sometimes it's difficult to differentiate between an enlarged uterus secondary to fibroids or secondary to adenomyosis."

"Why didn't you confirm your diagnosis before operating?"

I was getting defensive, could feel my face getting flushed. "I operated because of her clinical symptoms—"

"What symptoms, Doctor?" He was smiling.

"Pain, . . . ah, . . . pressure—"

"You can't remember what tests you ordered, but you do remember the patient's symptoms. How interesting." His smile became a smirk.

I wanted to scream in rage. I was losing this oral combat, and my opponent was laughing at me.

"I can't exactly remember too much about this patient—"

"Doctor Gehring, it appears you took this patient

directly from your examining table to the operating table, and the pathologist proved your diagnosis wrong—"

"That's not true—"

"Then tell us what is true, Doctor."

I couldn't. I couldn't remember too much about that patient; in fact, I couldn't remember too much about anything. My mind was foggy from the drugs, but I needed more. I was under attack; I needed to relax.

"Is there a bathroom close by?" I asked.

"Surely, Doctor. It's time for a break anyway. Let's reconvene here in about fifteen minutes."

In the bathroom I swallowed a handful of pills. I felt better even before the pills had time to work. I was euphoric knowing that soon I would be euphoric. They couldn't hurt me now.

They tore me apart.

I received a registered letter notifying me of my failure the same day Carolyn entered the hospital to have our baby. I knew that forty percent of applicants failed their oral board exams, but that was no consolation. I had never failed a test before.

I could still practice OB-Gyn—board certification was not a prerequisite for hospital privileges, and I could always be reexamined the next year. But I wanted that certificate to hang on my wall now—I wanted that status. And I hated failing. I was severely depressed.

"You can take that test anytime," Carolyn said. "Today is the birthday of your baby. It's a happy occasion. Put the test behind you. Cheer up."

I did exactly that. I wrote a prescription for Percodan and presented it to a pharmacist I knew. "Carolyn's having a baby by Cesarean section. She'll need these when she gets home."

The pharmacist filled the prescription. "You know that I shouldn't fill a 'script' for a schedule-II narcotic for you or your family, but I will. I know you, Dr. Gehring, and I know you won't abuse these drugs."

"Of course not," I said, clutching the bottle of Percodan. Carolyn's C-section went well, and the Percodan obliterated the pain of my failure. I was happy, garrulous, and excited.

Courtney Robin Gehring was born at 2:54 P.M. on March 7, 1979. I looked at her pretty little face; I saw the dimple in her chin (just like mine); I held her warm little body in my arms.

Parents had told me that seeing your baby for the first time gave you a feeling that was beyond description. Pediatricians called this feeling part of the bonding process, but they couldn't describe it either. When I held Courtney in my arms for the first time, I felt a warmth, a closeness, a protectiveness that I had never experienced before. It was a euphoria far superior to that generated by any drug.

I escorted Carolyn to the recovery room and waited until she fell asleep. Next I called our friends and relatives to tell them of the birth. Then I persuaded the nursery personnel to push Courtney's warmer to a remote corner of the nursery—away from the other babies. "We need to talk in private," I joked.

I sat silently on a stool and watched this new person for over an hour. Courtney was flailing her arms and legs—trying them out, as babies do. I studied her little fingers and toes, her protuberant tummy, her healthy pink cheeks. A thousand thoughts bombarded my consciousness. Future thoughts, past thoughts, baby thoughts, father thoughts.

I started talking to her in a soft whisper. "Happy birthday, little honey. Welcome to our world. We've got problems, to be sure, but it's not a bad world. There's still war and crime and starvation, but that's none of your concern, because your daddy will protect you from all that.

"I'll try to guide your life so that you'll see the beauty of our world. There are fuzzy little animals and sunsets and flowers. There's music and poetry and . . . well, I could just go on and on. You'll have all that, Courtney. I promise. I'll protect you."

Tears were streaming down my cheeks as I lifted her from the warmer and pressed her tiny body against mine. "Your daddy has a problem right now, little honey. He's gotten into something that he can't get out of. He's in way over his head. There's a beast inside of him that's consuming him. But that's not your concern. Your daddy's strong. Because of you, your daddy will kill that beast, and that beast will never threaten us again. I promise. I'll protect you."

At that moment, I wanted my own mom and dad to kill the beast for me. I wanted them to protect me; I wanted them to tell me that everything would be okay.

"Mom, Dad, God, somebody! Help me. You didn't tell me life would be so hard. You told me about teddy bears, love, marriage, children, and happiness. You didn't tell me about the rat race or the goddess of success who demands continual sacrifice or the alcohol or the drugs. You said I would live happily ever after.

"Now I have a child of my own to protect. But who will protect me? How can I give this child a happy life when mine is so miserable?

"Make me a little child again, and hold me close. Hold me like I'm holding this child. Kill the beast for me—make everything okay. Help me, Mom. Help me, Dad, . . . God, . . . somebody! Life is too hard—I can't do it alone anymore."

My new psychiatrist agreed. "You can't do it alone. I know. I'm a recovering alcoholic myself."

"How'd you get well?" I asked.

"Through Alcoholics Anonymous, and I'd suggest the same for you."

"No, thanks. I've tried AA. I went there thinking they had the answer to my addiction, but all they talked about was God."

He smiled. "God *is* the answer to our addiction. That's the basis for the whole program."

"But that's too vague. I can't see how the church . . ."

"Ah, you're making the same mistake I did. I confused God with organized religion. If you read AA's twelve steps, you'll notice it says *God as you understand Him.* It says nothing about the church."

"But that's the hooker. If I can understand God, then He's not the God that created the mysteries of the universe. He's too simple. The God that I believe in is complex enough to create black holes. . . ."

"You've created a catch-22. You're like Groucho Marx. He wouldn't join a country club that would accept him as a member. Let me put it as simply as I can. If your God is smart enough to create black holes, then he's smart enough to deliver you from your addiction."

"I can accept that. But there's another factor. I don't want to be seen at an AA meeting. What if somebody sees me. What about my reputation?"

"It's an anonymous group."

"I can't take that chance. I have a large, lucrative OB-Gyn practice."

"There are many doctors in AA. They'll tell you that their practices haven't suffered. But that's not the point. Even if your practice does decline, AA may save your life. What's more important?"

"My life, obviously. But I want to get out of this addiction and retain my practice and reputation. You know other doctors that are addicted?"

"Of course, did you think you were the only one?"

"Yes. And I'm surprised you admit your addiction."

"M.D.'s have the highest addiction rate of any of the professions. Addiction is an occupational hazard for us. If you won't consider AA, would you consider forming a group of addicted physicians?"

"Sure. If they're in the same boat I am, I think I can be sure of retaining my anonymity."

"Of course. Let me make a few calls. We'll arrange a meeting." He paused to light his pipe. "Tell me about your new baby."

"She's beautiful," I said flatly. "She's the best thing I've ever done."

"You don't seem too happy about it."

"I'm excited, of course. But I thought the baby would give me the push I needed—the impetus to stop drugs forever."

"Did you try to stop?"

"Yes. I started taking Percodan the day she was born. I told you about failing the board exams. The Percodan pulled me out of that depression. . . ."

"Of course it did. Narcotics work very effectively as mood elevators—if you're willing to pay the price of addiction. What happened when you tried to stop?"

"I wanted to kill myself. The depression was overwhelming. And I had physical symptoms. . . ."

"Withdrawal?"

"Severe."

"How many Percodan are you taking?"

"Just a few," I lied.

"I can't deal with answers like that. A few won't give you physical withdrawal. Please be honest, Bob. What's a few? Six? Ten?"

"About twenty-four a day." I expected an expletive, a grimace, a reprimand. Some kind of reaction. He merely sucked his pipe.

"You need hospitalization," he said.

"I knew you'd say that," I said angrily. "That's absolutely out of the question. You're not going to admit me to some nut house—"

"I wasn't talking about a nut house—"

"I'll kick this habit alone—"

"You said you couldn't do it alone."

"—without the help of the weirdos in a psych unit. I'll do it for Courtney. I'll make her proud of her daddy."

"Bob, whenever I tried to quit drinking for my wife or my children or for anybody else, I failed. You have to do it for yourself. You have a disease more lethal than cancer. Why not seek the help of specialists?"

"I'm not buying that disease crap. It's will power, pure and simple. I can't afford a hospital—what about my practice? Who's going to take care of my patients?"

"Who's taking care of them now? Certainly not you. Not on twenty-four Percodan a day. Or haven't you thought about that?"

"Of course I have. You have no idea of the guilt I'm carrying. But my patients would get worse care if I didn't take the pills. Believe me, I've tried. I get so terribly depressed I can't function. . . ."

"You've got the worst case of denial I've ever seen." He glanced at his watch. "Our hour is up; . . . I'll give you a call, and we'll arrange a meeting with other addicted doctors. In the meantime, I suggest you get down on your knees and pray."

"To whom?" I said.

Denial? What did he mean by that? What did he want? As far as I was concerned, I wasn't denying anything. I admitted that I was a pill freak, a junkie. I was completely honest. Well, almost. I couldn't tell anyone about sticking a needle in my body, not even him. And after all, that had happened only once. Couldn't he understand? The drugs were my salvation. Life was too miserable without them.

On a rainy Wednesday night in March 1979, my psychiatrist and I met with several other addicted physicians in the old YMCA building in downtown Dallas. Some, like myself, were still actively using drugs; some had been clean and sober for years.

"You need hospitalization," a radiologist told me. I told him I couldn't afford it.

"You need God," a psychiatrist said. I told him I'd heard that before.

"You need a swift kick in the pants," a surgeon said. I couldn't argue with that.

"You're in full-blown denial," the surgeon continued. (*That word again!*) "You have a warehouse full of persuasive arguments to continue your addiction. So did I. I just wish I had stopped at the pill stage. But I didn't. After the pills didn't work any more, I started injecting morphine—shooting up, mainlining, . . . anything you want to call it. I lost it all—my family, my reputation, my practice, even my medical license.

"You're fortunate, Doctor," he continued. "You're seeking help at the pill stage of your addiction. You're catching it early. Let me give you a word of advice. Give it your best shot. *Now!* Get into a hospital, get right with God, turn your whole life around. Because I'm telling you, unless you do, you won't stop with just the pills. You'll be using needles, too. It doesn't matter how you get the drugs into your bloodstream, the results are the same. You have a progressive disease—"

"Disease?" I interrupted. "How can intelligent men of medicine call this weakness a disease? Disease is a cop-out. We can't justify our irrational behavior, so we say we have a disease. How convenient. Show me the lesion in my brain that compels me to use drugs at all costs, and then I might believe you. Until then, I must revert to the scientific training we all had in medical school—and I can't remember anything about the disease of addiction. But that's all I've heard—disease and denial."

"And you have both," the doctors said.

We closed the meeting with the Lord's Prayer and decided to meet again the following Wednesday night. I departed with ambivalent feelings about this group. I had always felt uncomfortable with other doctors—their country-club chat, stock-market analysis, and latest hot diagnosis left me cold. But these men were different. They were honest and sincere, and they talked about feelings instead of the

Dow Jones. They were concerned about me and my addiction. I liked them.

But I was also looking for an answer from this brain trust. I wanted three easy steps out of my addiction, and they couldn't give me that. They could advise me about the necessity for hospitals and Alcoholics Anonymous and God. They could meet with me and talk with me. I saw no therapeutic value in their advice, their meetings, or their talk.

Nevertheless, I went back the following Wednesday night. It was the same group minus one. He had committed himself to a hospital. They strongly urged that I join him, and I refused. I couldn't afford it, I said.

Several days later, I came home after taking an adequate dose of Percodan to get me through the evening. I searched for the remote-control switch for the television set but couldn't find it. I turned the living room upside down in my quest. Why didn't the kids leave it where it was supposed to be? Why were people trying to sabotage me? There were times during that ten-to-fifteen-minute search when I had to sit down and ask myself just exactly what I was looking for. Oh, yes, the remote-control switch. I would then begin my frantic effort anew. I was dizzy, confused.

Finally my stepson, Gary, asked, "What are you looking for?"

"The remote-control switch. Have you seen it?"

I will never forget the expression on his little face. It was a composite of fear, concern, and bewilderment. He had just watched me tear the living room apart looking for a television switch that was sitting directly in front of me.

"It's right in front of you," Gary said.

"Where?"

He went to the coffee table and pointed. "Here."

"So it is. Did you just put it there?"

"It's been there all the time."

"Don't lie to me," I shouted. "I know you were hiding it."

His lower lip was quivering in fear. "I didn't hide it. . . ."

"Gary, if it had been on the table the whole time, I would have found it. I'm tired of your silly little games and your lying." The child was now sobbing uncontrollably. "Now go to your room."

I knew that Gary hadn't hidden it. I knew that I was too drugged to see it, too drugged to know what I was doing. I was out of control. But my medical training paid off handsomely. "When you're wrong, don't admit it." Unfortunately, my drug addiction was not only destroying me, it was destroying my family. While I sat crying in my bedroom, Gary was crying in his. I was truly frightened. For the first time, I was so drugged that I didn't know what I was doing.

The following day I admitted myself to St. Luke's Hospital in Phoenix, Arizona. (There were excellent alcohol and drug hospitals in Dallas, but I didn't want anyone to know.) I told my office staff that my father was sick, and I had to visit him in North Dakota. I told the truth to only one of my three OB-Gyn partners. He was surprised at my admission of drug addiction. As I related the severity of my problem, I expected him to throw me out of his office in disgust and ask me to resign from the partnership. Instead he said, "Bob, you're a good doctor and a good friend. I love you, and I'll pray for you. Take as much time as you need. I'll take care of things here."

I arrived at St. Luke's in severe withdrawal. I was cramping and sweating and going to the bathroom every ten minutes. I became impatient with the nurse taking my history.

"What drugs are you addicted to?"

"Everything in the *PDR*." (*Physician's Desk Reference:* a compendium of all prescription drugs.)

"Can you be more specific?"

"Alcohol, marijuana, Darvon, codeine, Fiorinal—"

"Okay, okay." She wrote "polydrug abuser" on my history form.

"Any serious medical or surgical illnesses?"

"Is there a bathroom close by?" I asked.

"Of course, around the corner and to your right."

We finished the history with the inevitable and standard questions. "Have you ever thought about suicide?" Yes. "Have you ever planned your suicide?" No.

I didn't tell her of my impulse to open the emergency door of the aircraft and leap to my death. They weren't going to lock me in a padded cell.

My doctor and I had much in common. He was an ex-OB-Gyn man who had kicked a Percodan habit himself. He saw that I was in withdrawal and ordered methadone to ease the discomfort.

"I'll gradually decrease the dosage of methadone until you're drug free. It's very humane. You don't need the punishment of withdrawal, you've been punished enough."

After that initial high dose of methadone, I was happy and excited about my recovery. I told the other patients that we were indeed fortunate to be in a clean, orderly environment to recover from the madness of our addictions. We were under the care of specialists, and if we cooperated, these good doctors would make us well. I was Dr. Pollyanna.

Then they started reducing my dose of methadone. At the end of a week I was drug free and miserable. I couldn't eat, sleep, or communicate. I withdrew to my room and stared at the walls.

Initially I didn't say much in group therapy; I was too ashamed. (Unlike my first experience with group therapy, this time I was no observer; I was a full-fledged member!) Finally the therapist asked how I was doing, and through the tears, I spilled out my guilt and despair. "I'm a doctor, and I'm in a hospital for drug addiction. Would you send your wife or mother or sister to a doctor like me? I'm a medical doctor; I should know better."

A woman in the group brought a box of Kleenex over to me, then sat in the chair beside me. She told me that doctoring was only my occupation. She said I was a child of God just like she was, and I should give myself a break. "You're merely a human being," she said, "and humans are imperfect. God has forgiven you; try to forgive yourself." I hugged her. I hadn't hugged anyone except Carolyn in years. It felt good.

To pass the time, I went to occupational therapy and made leather belts. Belts for Carolyn. Belts for the kids. The gifted hands of a gynecological surgeon making leather belts. I took out all my frustrations on those belts. I didn't realize my own intensity until one day I glanced up to see the other patients watching me and smiling. One said, "Bob, I hope you don't operate the way you make belts. I'd pity your poor patients." I joined their laughter.

One night a man entered my room, introduced himself, and began talking. He told me he was a doctor and was just visiting the hospital because he needed to talk to another addicted doctor. He had been a patient here some time back and found it therapeutic to converse with other junkies like himself. He straddled a chair and began a humorous narrative that had me in stitches in spite of my gloom.

"I was a good Jewish boy with a good Jewish mother who fed me as if we had just escaped from Auschwitz. I was a fat kid—a compulsive overeater. But that was just the beginning of many compulsive habits."

He told me about losing that weight and finding another compulsion—gambling. "Not penny-ante stuff, mind you. Thousands of dollars on the roll of the dice. The casinos in Vegas loved to see me coming. I had to bet big—thousands of dollars. For it to be exciting, it had to hurt when I lost. And believe me, it hurt.

"Then drugs. Amphetamines to lose weight, then narcotics, needles, cocaine, morphine, you name it. I was kicked out of three hospitals for my addiction. I even took birth-control pills until my voice squeaked and I had this strange compulsion to buy silk underwear."

In a short time I had forgotten my problems and was laughing with him. "How can you be so flippant about all this . . . ?"

"Oh, I used to wallow in the guilt. I suppose you're

wallowing. We all do. But Christ has absorbed the guilt. Christ just told me one day that I had enough to worry about so why didn't I just let him handle the guilt problems—"

"I beg your pardon?"

"Jesus Christ. You know, the Messiah—"

"But you're Jewish."

"I know. That's what my parents keep saying. They weren't too happy when I became a Christian. But He saved my life. So much for preaching. How are you doing? Bet you can't sleep, can you?"

"How'd you know?"

"I couldn't either when I was withdrawing. But you're in luck. I brought a sleeping pill with me—"

"I can't, . . . really. I'm trying to—"

"Don't get excited. The pill is called prayer. You know how to pray, don't you?"

"I think so—"

"Well, get down on your knees and join me." He knelt beside the bed.

"If you don't mind, I'll just sit here on the bed and—"

"Get down on your knees, Bob. It does us all a great deal of good to humble ourselves before a power greater than ourselves. Especially we doctors. We're so used to playing gods ourselves that it's refreshing to turn it over to the real God. . . ."

I knelt beside him. He was right. It did feel good to get on my knees. His prayer was totally for me—he mentioned nothing about himself. He prayed about my addiction, my family, my future. He prayed that I would sleep soundly.

Amazingly, for the first time in weeks, I did. What an odd coincidence.

I was being bombarded with God from all sides. The lecturers told me about the disease concept again. They told me that I was genetically predisposed to addiction. I had been born with my disease. I was biochemically different from other people. I didn't react to mood-altering chemicals the way normal people did. (I could certainly attest to that.)

That explained how I became addicted. That was the way in. The way out was through God. A Hindu God, a Buddhist God, a Jewish God, a Christian God. It didn't matter, they said. A Higher Power—a power greater than yourself.

My first psychiatrist told me that God was the answer, so did the second. The recovering doctors in our group said so. The converted Jewish doctor, the specialists in the hospital—they all said the same thing. I wasn't dumb. Maybe I should listen for a change.

I began reading the numerous AA pamphlets that were lying around the unit. One was about a hopeless drunk who asked God to deliver him from his alcoholism, and immediately he felt a strong wind and saw a blinding light in his room. I attributed all that to hallucinations he was having during his d.t.'s. But the man never drank again. God had given him a sign.

That's what I needed! A sign from God! Not a big sign, just something to let me know He was there. I prayed and nothing happened.

Shortly before I was to be discharged, a group of us from the hospital attended an anniversary celebration of the founding of Alcoholics Anonymous in Phoenix. About two thousand people met in a large convention hall. There were free drinks (nonalcoholic, of course), entertainment, and door prizes.

Door prizes. That's it. Here's your chance, God. Show me you exist. Let me win a door prize. I don't care what prize. It's not the prize; it's the fact that I'm going to pray to win one, and you're going to prove your existence. That prize will be my blinding light.

There were ten door prizes. I bought ten tickets. Two thousand people each buying ten tickets for ten door prizes. Fat chance.

When the woman began reading the winning numbers, I started praying. "God, I know it's a silly request, but it's important for me. I need a sign. You gave Moses a burning bush, give me a door prize. Please."

Seven numbers were called and seven prizes were given away. Then eight. She started the ninth number, and I couldn't believe it. I had the ticket! God was real! I had a sign!

I rushed up to the stage with my winning ticket.

"You won a card table with four chairs."

"It doesn't matter," I said.

"What doesn't matter?" she said.

"It doesn't matter what I won. God is real!"

She looked at me with a patronizing expression that said, "Poor brain-damaged alcoholic. And so young, too." Aloud she said, "Of course He is, young man. Congratulations."

Back at the hospital, I told some of the other patients about the sign from God. They all listened in polite silence; then I heard a snicker, a few giggles, and finally raucous laughter.

"Bob, I need a new car. Think you can swing it?"

My face turned red in embarrassment. "Admittedly, it sounds far-fetched, but—"

"Think you can part the Red Sea?"

"Why settle for a card table and four chairs. You're on a roll. Try for a million dollars."

I excused myself and went to my room. They were right. It was merely a coincidence. God doesn't give card tables as signs. I called Carolyn and told her what had happened.

"There are no coincidences with God," she said. "Please believe that He gave you that table, and He'll give you much, much more if you'll only ask Him."

I didn't believe, and I didn't ask for more. God was still an indifferent cosmic force. I was embarrassed that even for a moment I had believed in that silly, selfish prayer. Fate rolled the dice, and my number came up. Nothing more. Three plums lined up on the celestial slot machine, and I won a card table. Big deal.

St. Luke's discharged me after twenty-nine days. I could tell they weren't too optimistic, but I assured them that I had "learned my lesson" and would never be back. My doctor winced and said that if I viewed my hospitalization as a lesson that needed to be learned, then I missed the whole point of my hospitalization. "Learn your lesson" was tantamount to punishment, and I wasn't there to be punished but to bury the old and begin the new. A new life, a changed life—that's what their program was all about. I still wanted to punish myself.

They gave me a medallion that said "Surrender to Win." Surrender was alien to me. My pseudomilitary leanings told me that surrender and win were opposites, incompatible, incongruous. That motto sounded too much like the teachings of Jesus Christ. Didn't Christ teach to turn the other cheek? That the first shall be last, and the last first? To become as a little child? Blessed are the meek? That's fine on paper. A beautiful philosophy, indeed, but totally unrealistic in modern technological society. The meek don't fare well in the jungle of the twentieth century.

Sure, I had to surrender to my addiction. I knew that. I could never underestimate the power drugs had over me. The drugs had beaten me. I gave up. I surrendered. They won.

But the specialists wanted me to surrender my life and my will and my soul. I couldn't do that. And if I could, whom would I surrender it to? Who was there to receive it? And what would I win?

I came home and resumed my practice. ("My father is doing much better, thank you.") I wasn't drinking or drugging. I went to work and I came home. I was either angry or depressed. I didn't go to AA meetings; I didn't see my psychiatrists; I didn't pray. I did attend the doctor's group on Wednesdays, but offered little to them and received less in return. I was totally miserable.

Years later, I would learn what those dark days had meant for Carolyn and my family. . . .

"I was so excited when Bob returned home from the hospital," Carolyn said. "I wasn't naive enough to think that he was cured—by then I knew there was no cure for his problem. But he did seem confident of his recovery. For a period of time he participated in family activities, developed outside interests, and exercised. I even talked him into attending church one Sunday. I asked what he thought of the service, and he said something about 'It bore no relevance to the twentieth century.' That ended that. However, he did call that silly card table his God table, so I knew there must be a spark of spirituality in him, however small.

"His new zeal for living was short-lived. I soon saw the look of defeat on his face again. Please understand, I never considered Bob a weak man. He wasn't. His life was proof of his determination and strength. A midwestern farm kid, Vietnam veteran, medical school graduate, and then a successful big-city doctor. He was accustomed to tackling insurmountable tasks and winning. He was a dynamic, take-charge individual. But he placed such unrealistic demands on himself.

"So when I saw that defeated look again, I knew we were in for trouble. It seemed he was ashamed that there was something in his life that had whipped him—his drug addiction. He gradually relinquished all decision making to me. I paid the bills, handled the money, took care of the family. . . . When I did ask him for advice on a particular problem, he would say 'You handle it, Carolyn. Do what you think is right.' His only interest that summer of 1979 was Courtney; our baby brought him great happiness, but only for brief periods at a time. He would play with her for a while, then retreat to the bedroom—alone. He even ate his meals there. The children and I had to function without him.

"Weekends were terrible. He would make rounds and then sit for the rest of the day. Just sit. And stare. And cry.

"Many nights he would lie in bed and stare at the ceiling. He would cry and eventually blurt out 'Why are you doing this to me, God? Why are you killing me? Why do you want to destroy me? What have I done wrong? If you want me dead so badly, give me cancer or a heart attack. But not this slow, insidious, painful torture. Do it quickly, for God's sake; do it quickly.'

"I didn't know what to do. Encouragement didn't even help any more. I had said everything dozens of times. I frequently just cried with him. I shared his torment. But I couldn't help him. I knew no human power could ever help him.

"Then, sometime in September of 1979, I noticed a miraculous change in him. He became cheerful, considerate, and personable. His energy was boundless. Even our friends noticed that he was pulling out of his depression. My prayers had been answered.

"I invited an old friend and her husband to dinner one night. Bob was the perfect host, and they both commented on how sweet and charming he was. My old Bob was back again.

"Of course I thought about drugs. I was suspicious because a happy Bob usually meant a drugged Bob. I jokingly confronted him, searching for the truth. At first he angrily denied any drug use. Sensing that his anger only confirmed my suspicions, he then pleasantly thanked me for the compliment. 'I'm not taking drugs, but I'm honored that you would think I am,' he said. 'It just proves that I can be as happy without drugs as I can with them.' He was very convincing—the consummate con artist. But I wanted so desperately to believe him. I wanted him to be really happy again.

"Then he began to spend more time away from home. On weekends I hardly saw him at all. When he said he was at the hospital, I didn't question him. His practice was still quite large. And I had my own little world—three children and the full family responsibilities that Bob had abandoned. I was busy too.

"His behavior became more and more erratic. He began wearing long-sleeved shirts all the time. In Texas it's still pretty hot in September and October, and there he was—sweating in his long-sleeved shirts with the cuffs buttoned. He never even rolled up the sleeves. I casually mentioned that he would be more comfortable in a summer shirt. He said that none of them fit. Well, I knew that wasn't true; at that time he hadn't gained or lost any weight, but I bought him some new ones anyway. When he wore them, I noticed what appeared to be a thin film of my cosmetics on his arms. 'It's just a rash, Carolyn,' he said. 'It's ugly, and I'm just covering it up.' He had an answer for everything, but I was getting that sick feeling again.

"We started getting weird things in the mail. One package contained a mushroom farm, a pair of weird-looking glasses made of prisms, designed to allow a person to lie flat on his back and still see the TV set, and flashlights. Lots of flashlights. Key-chain flashlights, 5-cell flashlights, 2-cell flashlights, a flashlight with a screwdriver attached to the front, even a car key with a built-in light. Bob had ordered all these things from the little junk catalogs we received. After I went to bed, he would stay up ordering junk. If it hadn't been so tragic, it would have been humorous.

"I knew he was on drugs again, but I had no proof. The things I confronted him about were merely answered in his usual logical way. I knew he was lying, but what could I do?

"I asked his office staff about his behavior. 'Nothing unusual,' they said. 'Tired perhaps, but aren't all doctors? How's his ear infection?' I knew nothing about an ear infection. 'Well,' his nurse said, 'I had to cancel the whole day because he was so dizzy. Said his equilibrium was disturbed by an inner-ear problem. But nothing unusual.'

"Ear infection? He had an answer for everything. One night I was cleaning the bathroom and stepped on something hard under the bathroom rug. I lifted the rug and found an empty syringe. I started crying. It wasn't pills anymore—it was syringes and needles. I tearfully showed Bob the evidence and pleaded with him to get help before it got any worse. Again he had an answer. Yes, he had used a syringe but it was only for an antibiotic for a sore throat. Why hadn't his nurse given him the shot? He didn't want to bother her. Why didn't he give himself the shot at the office instead of at home? He didn't have the correct antibiotic at the office—he had to stop at a pharmacy. Why did he hide the syringe under the rug? He was going to dispose of it later but simply forgot. 'What is this, the Spanish Inquisition? Get off my case.' I cried all night.

"I needed help, but who could I talk to? His drug problem was a big secret. I knew some of the doctors in his recovery group, but I knew Bob could convincingly lie to them, too. He was quite intimidating, and I had no real proof.

"I noticed that he made frequent trips to his car, so I got up early one morning while he was still sleeping and turned that car inside out. No drugs. One day my son, Gary, was playing outside and came in with a syringe in his hand. He said he found it in the bushes and asked what it was. I gave him a feeble explanation, went upstairs, and presented the syringe to Bob. 'Gary found it in the bushes,' I said. 'So?' he replied. End of discussion.

"I knew I would need irrefutable evidence. A smoking gun, so to speak. Anything less than that would give him the opportunity to lie his way out again. I couldn't take that chance. What would I do if he ever overdosed? He'd be dead in minutes.

"I watched through the window as he made one of his trips to the car. I could see his silhouette against the trunk light. He lifted something up, glanced back at the house, then hurriedly stuck something in his jacket pocket. Of course, how stupid of me! The drugs were hidden in the spare tire compartment of his trunk. He came back into the house, went to the closet, and then locked himself in the bathroom.

"After he went to sleep, I searched the closet. The loaded syringes were in the inside coat pockets of his suits. I left them there and went to his car. Carefully hidden under the spare tire were more loaded syringes and a bottle labeled Dilaudid. I felt a little ashamed, spying on my husband, doing all this clandestine detective work, but at least now I had the evidence. Maybe now he would get help.

"The next day I called a friend who was a registered nurse and asked her about Dilaudid. 'It's morphine, Carolyn,' she said. 'Dilaudid is the strongest narcotic known to medicine. It's only used for terminal cancer patients or severe postoperative pain. Why do you ask?' 'No particular reason,' I said. 'Bob just mentioned he had a patient who had an allergic reaction to Dilaudid, and I had never heard of it before. Is it addicting?' 'Oh, yes. Highly addicting,' she said.

"That evening I confronted Bob with the bottle of Dilaudid and all the syringes. He wasn't angry; in fact, he seemed relieved. The lying was over, he said. He needed help, but he would not go back to the hospital. Yes, he was physically addicted. Yes, he would go through withdrawal. Yes, he would get sick, but he wasn't going to be locked up again. We had to keep this a secret. He would give me all his drugs and I would gradually decrease his dosage until he was off. 'But I'm not a nurse,' I said. 'I know nothing about drugs.' That's okay. He would tell me all I needed to know. I bought it, hook, line, and sinker.

"After several days it was apparent that he was conning me again. I made sure he took the decreasing dosage according to plan, and I expected him to start going through the physical withdrawal. He didn't. It was obvious he was adding a little of his own Dilaudid to the dosage I measured out for him. I became very angry.

"You're a typical junkie con artist. You lie, cheat, and steal. Your drugs are more important to you than me, your baby, or even your life. You're shooting up the strongest narcotic invented. What's next? Heroin? (I didn't know that Dilaudid was the equivalent of heroin.) Soon you'll be robbing drug stores. . . .

"That evening he locked himself in the bathroom. He was in there for the longest time. I knocked and he didn't reply. I started crying and pleaded with him to come out, to at least say something so I'd know he was alive. He finally came out and barely made it to the bed before he collapsed. His body was drenched in sweat. Blood was dripping from his arm. In panic I called one of the doctors in his group, and he and another doctor were at our door within an hour. 'I'm not going to the nut house again,' Bob screamed. 'I'll withdraw myself, but I will not be incarcerated.'

"They very calmly told him to be realistic. They said that he could con and lie to his wife and everyone else, but not to other junkies. 'We've been there, Bob,' they told him. 'We know all the tricks and mind games. You can't withdraw yourself, and you know it, so can the crap!'

"God bless those men. Bob listened to them. Even in his drugged state of mind, he knew he couldn't fool another drug addict. He finally agreed to hospitalization, but only someplace close to Dallas. 'I want Carolyn to be with me as much as possible.' I just prayed that this time it would end.

"I drove him to an alcohol and drug hospital in Fort Worth. He was in withdrawal before we even got there. We sat in the parking lot of the hospital, and he asked me to step out of the car for a minute. He had one syringe left and was going to use it to ward off the withdrawal for as long as possible. I left him in the car that dark night to use the last of his drugs. (He never injected himself in front of me. He was too ashamed.) His doctor-addict friends had told me to let him use all the drugs he wanted to before admission. Let the hospital staff take care of his withdrawal. I followed their advice.

"I got him admitted and drove back to Dallas. The next time I saw him he was writhing in pain. Sweat was pouring from his face. His eyes were swollen shut. He didn't even know I was in the room. The nurse gave him a shot and he relaxed. He then noticed me. 'Thank God, Carolyn, you're here,' he said. He kept repeating something about 'I think

I've destroyed my kidneys. My kidneys are gone. The drugs have destroyed my kidneys.' Then he fell asleep.

"I asked the nurse what he meant about his kidneys. She said that Bob was concerned about his swollen eyes and puffy face. Yes, he had damaged his kidneys, but they certainly weren't destroyed. In light of everything, she added, he's lucky to be alive. The amount of Dilaudid he was using was ten times the lethal dose. It would have killed most people.

"As I drove home, I cried and prayed like I had never prayed before. It isn't fair, God. It just isn't fair. Bob Gehring is a good person, God. He's never purposely hurt anyone in his whole life. He's gentle and kind. Please make him well. 'Create in him a clean heart, O God, and renew a right spirit within him. Cast him not away from thy presence, and take not thy Holy Spirit from him. Restore unto him the joy of thy salvation, and sustain him with a willing spirit . . .

"Please do those things for him, God. And for me, too. Amen."

THE VALLEY OF THE SHADOW OF DEATH

Dilaudid and Cocaine

Was I aware that my behavior was bizarre? Yes. In fact, I was more acutely aware of my erratic actions than those around me. There was no rational way I could explain my preoccupation with junk catalogs, mushroom farms, and flashlights. I knew it was drug-induced insanity.

I avoided looking in the mirror. I had lost weight precipitously, and my clothing hung loosely on my emaciated frame. My color was chalk-white. But it was my eyes that frightened me most. They had a glazed, vacant stare. My eyelids were large black bags. If I could see that look, others could, too. Direct eye contact was out of the question.

Because the drugs made me perspire heavily and the sunlight hurt my eyes, I kept the bedroom intolerably cold and dark. I was like a living dead man.

Did I know I was lying to Carolyn and others? Yes, and I think that hurt the most. I had always been proud of my honesty. But drug addiction and honesty were incompatible. How could I admit that my life was so unbearable that I had resorted to sticking needles in my veins? It was too shameful—the guilt was too overwhelming.

A day before my second hospitalization, a pharmacist called the office to check on a prescription for Dilaudid that I had written for my mother-in-law (and used myself). My OB-Gyn partner overheard my nurse okaying the prescription.

"Is your mother-in-law sick?" he asked.

181

"Oh, yes," I replied.

"She must be," added another office worker. "We've had several calls to check on Dilaudid prescriptions for her."

"Are you her doctor, Bob?" my partner asked.

"Yes, . . . well, actually no," I replied. "I just give her some pain meds to get her over the hump. She always gets better. . . ."

"But Dilaudid? Can't she take something milder?"

"She's allergic to almost everything—believe me, I've tried her on almost every pain pill . . ."

I knew I was lying. (Again, no eye contact.) He knew I was lying. The sad thing is—I knew he knew I was lying, but I couldn't force myself to admit the truth.

"Are you doing okay, Bob? Is this something we should talk about?"

Looking directly over his shoulder, I answered, "Couldn't be better, sir." I felt my face burn with embarrassment. (*I know you're a good friend, and I know you're concerned about me. And I know that you know I'm using drugs again. But if I tell you the truth, you'll take my drugs away. I can't bear that. I can't live without those drugs. Please understand, I HAVE to lie to you.*)

Did I know I couldn't practice medicine and use drugs at the same time? Did I know that I would lose my practice? Did I know that I would eventually lose my medical license? Yes. After that first intravenous injection of Dilaudid, I knew there was no turning back. I knew I would lose my practice and eventually my medical license.

When I started back on the pills in September, 1979— only four miserable months after my discharge from St. Luke's—I knew I couldn't take any mood-altering drugs again. Mentally, I had acknowledged that before I left the hospital. But what about the terrible headaches I got everyday? If a patient needed relief from incapacitating headaches, wouldn't I prescribe something? And one Darvon wasn't drug addiction. I was merely treating a headache. One Darvon wouldn't interfere with my practice.

Within a week I was taking up to thirty Percodan a day, but those binges were on weekends and times when I wasn't on call. I could still practice medicine on a much lower dose—just enough to ward off the physical withdrawal. Even on the reduced dosage of drugs that I used during office hours, I knew my judgment was impaired. I sought consults for anything more serious than routine office visits. I was no longer practicing medicine—I relied on other doctors to make important decisions for me. In retrospect, it was only by the grace of God that I didn't hurt a patient. I could have very easily. I was dangerous.

But even thirty Percodan a day couldn't assuage the demons within me. The surgeon in our Wednesday group had said, "It doesn't matter how you get the drugs into your bloodstream, the results are the same. It's a progressive disease; you'll be using needles, too." I progressed according to plan.

At first I only used the injections on weekends, and occasionally after office hours; but soon I shortened my office hours to accommodate my new friend, Dilaudid. Within weeks, I was showing up late, canceling individual appointments, then canceling complete days. I was too drugged to work.

No, my patients didn't know about the mushroom farm or the funny glasses. They didn't see the needle marks. (Carolyn's makeup worked wonders.) They weren't aware of the drugs I had used the night before. But they *were* aware of my appearance.

"Dr. Gehring, you look sick,. . . you've lost weight, . . . your eyes are . . . well, . . . funny. Are you okay?"

They were also aware of my nonappearance.

"No, Dr. Gehring is not in today. When do I expect him back? Well, I'm not really sure. He's been rather sick, you know. Yes, I know he canceled your appointment last week, too. Call again tomorrow."

And they were especially aware of my anger.

"Doesn't he ever smile anymore? He used to spend so

much time with me, and now he can't get rid of me fast enough."

"I will never see that man again. He told me never to question his medical knowledge. If I wanted to play doctor, then I needed to go to medical school just like he did. All I did was ask him a simple question. I don't need that abuse."

The anger was pervasive. Our home was about thirty minutes from the office on Interstate 30. Frequently, especially during rush hours, all lanes of traffic would be backed up for miles. Moving at a snail's pace was not my idea of fun, especially when I was in a hurry to get home to my drugs. Invariably there was always a person, usually driving a pickup truck, who would pull out onto the shoulder of the interstate, pass fifty cars, and then try to get back on the highway in front of me. I was mad enough anyway—now some jerk wanted to squeeze in ahead of me.

I would sit and stew, thump the steering wheel, and swear at the traffic and especially the driver who wanted to buck the line. I imagined the hood ornament on my car as the gun sight on a 105 mm howitzer that we used in Vietnam. I would align my gunsight directly on the pickup truck and mercilessly blast him off the face of the earth.

Rumors of my drug addiction were rampant. Patients started leaving me in droves. During my second hospitalization, I told my office staff to tell my patients that my father was sick again and I was in North Dakota visiting him. One patient remarked, "Well, I hope his father gets well soon, then maybe Dr. Gehring will stop taking those darned drugs." I wasn't fooling anyone.

Did I know that I was damaging my kidneys? Oh yes, and much more. As a medical doctor, I knew what I was doing to my body. I knew my lungs were damaged from filtering the sediment and particulate matter in the drugs I was injecting. Initially, I used only the sterile, pharmaceutical liquid, but I soon found that I could never explain the massive quantities of drugs as "office-use medications." So I began writing prescriptions for the Dilaudid tablets for fictitious patients. (More felony prescriptions.) The tablets were easier to obtain than the injectable liquid, but I then had to dissolve the tablets in water, filter, and then sterilize the solution. At first, I was meticulous about this whole process. Later, especially in the death throes of cocaine, I didn't bother to filter or sterilize. All that garbage was collecting in my lungs and kidneys.

I feared that the sediment and bacteria were being deposited on my heart valves. I knew about SBE (subacute bacterial endocarditis), and I knew that drug addicts were predisposed to this condition. In fact, a drug-addict patient of mine in medical school developed a staph septicemia with the resulting pneumonia and heart damage. He had to undergo open-heart surgery to replace his damaged heart valves—the bacteria had literally eaten them up. All of this secondary to dirty needles and contaminated drugs.

I knew about serum hepatitis, also common among drug addicts. I also knew the effects alcohol had had on my liver. I knew my liver couldn't withstand the constant bombardment of the myriad of chemicals I was ingesting and injecting.

I knew my veins were being scarred by the repeated needle jabs. I knew the chemicals were destroying brain cells. I knew I was dying.

I knew I would lose Carolyn and the kids. This devoted, understanding person who loved me so dearly could only tolerate so much. My drug addiction would eventually destroy her, too, unless she divorced herself from me and my first love.

During the course of my addiction, I repeatedly came home, covered in blood and vomit, and pleaded with Carolyn to take the kids and make a new life for themselves. "The drugs are killing me, Carolyn," I remember saying. "I know the drugs are killing me, but I can't stop. No matter how hard I try, I can't stop. Leave now, before it's too late— before your life is ruined, too. Can't you understand? I'm a dead man. It's just a matter of time."

"God will never let you die, Bob Gehring," she would say. "As long as you are trying, I will never leave you. We'll get out of this. I know we will. Just keep trying. We'll do it together."

I knew all those things. Most people think alcoholic drug addicts are oblivious to the consequences of their actions. We aren't.

I knew I would lose my reputation, my practice, my medical license, my family, my health, and eventually, my life. Those were the givens; they went with the territory.

Why then, couldn't I stop? Or after stopping, why did I always start again? I found myself directing the same questions to myself that I had addressed to the drug addicts in San Jose. I was a sane, rational man, but I found myself giving the same irrational answer that they did: "I don't know."

Were the needles a punishment for an undeserving life? Did I deserve the pain because I was such a worthless human being? Needles hurt. I was repulsed at the thought of using my body as a pin cushion. But there was the ultimate reward that followed the pain. And initially, the reward was worth the pain.

Was it for the reward, the euphoria of the drugs? There is no denying that narcotics make you feel good. They block all pain, both physical and psychic. They are highly effective as mood elevators. And initially they work one hundred percent of the time. But only initially. Soon even the drug reward wasn't working. I was crying before I used drugs, and I was crying after I used drugs. The drugs no longer pulled me out of the depression; in fact, they made it worse. I used drugs to treat my depression, but I knew drugs were wrong. That caused more guilt and depression, which I treated with more drugs, which caused more depression . . . ad infinitum. A vicious cycle that can only lead to death, because along with the depression, there was the physical addiction to be reckoned with. Long after the drugs stopped working as a mood elevator, I needed them in increasing dosages to combat the physical withdrawal. That wonderful euphoria at the end of the needle soon reached a point of diminishing returns. My best friend turned on me time after time.

Was it a death wish? Drug addiction is frequently described as slow suicide. There aren't any old junkies. I was a man who couldn't allow himself the luxury of making a mistake, a man who as a child destroyed a whole model airplane because he glued a piece in backward. Drug addiction was the ultimate mistake. My model airplane was ruined, my life in shambles. Why not destroy it?

But if I harbored a true death wish, why didn't I act on it sooner than I did? If I knew the drugs were killing me, why didn't I speed the process along? I didn't want to die, but I didn't want to live, either. People dying of a fatal disease hope for a miracle. In a strange way I hoped for that miracle, while doubting that miracles really happened.

Disinhibition euphoria? Self-flagellation? Delayed-stress syndrome from Vietnam? Death wish? I let the psychiatrists debate these issues. I only knew that there was no alternative—life was unbearable without drugs.

I stayed in that Fort Worth hospital for only three days. My doctor, a recovering Demerol addict himself, was incredulous and angry.

"You came in here tottering on the brink of death itself, and now you want to leave. I haven't even gotten you out of intensive care—you're not through the worst of your physical withdrawal. It'll take you weeks to get over the effects of that much Dilaudid. Think, man, think! Obviously I can't keep you here, but you'll have to sign out AMA [against medical advice]. I won't be a party to your destruction."

Two weeks later I was back in St. Luke's Alcohol and Drug Unit. "We've been expecting you," they said. "We knew you hadn't surrendered the last time. Of course, we'll get you off the drugs, but only God can keep you off them. Please listen to us this time."

My converted Jewish friend again came by to visit me. "We all bottom out, Bob. Some of us have high bottoms— we quit drugging before we lose everything. You're still in that category. You still have your family, medical license, home. . . . Maybe you haven't lost enough yet. Maybe you need to reach the low bottom category as I did. The scary thing, however, is that some people's bottom is death itself. They let the addiction overwhelm them—their only recourse is suicide. I have a feeling that you're overwhelmed. Christ can raise your bottom, Bob. Why don't you let him?"

I attended the required Narcotics Anonymous meetings at St. Luke's. Seven months earlier, during my first hospitalization, I had attended the NA meetings and felt totally out of place. Most of the members were bikers (Hells Angels types) and hookers—certainly not of my social caliber. After seven months, I found the same bikers and hookers. Only they were clean, and I was still drugging. They had found the handle, and I was still looking.

"Help me," I said.

"Sure, man," a biker said. "It's simple. Don't use drugs, pray, go to meetings, read the Big Book [of Alcoholics Anonymous], work the Twelve Steps, and change your whole life."

"I thought you said it was simple," I replied.

"Simple, man. I didn't say it was easy."

That same biker wrote a note in my Big Book before my discharge. "Don't be too smart to get well, man." (It seemed I had heard that before.) He added, "Except that ye be converted and become as little children, ye shall not enter the kingdom of heaven."

Christmas, 1979. I returned home with another Surrender-to-Win medallion. Americans were being held hostage in Iran. I was held hostage in Dallas.

By now the office staff and the other doctors knew of my drug addiction. One partner resigned. The other partners were empathic, but wanted assurance that I had buried my drug addiction once and for all. I didn't blame them. They had worked extra hard to cover my dwindling practice while I was hospitalized. There were legal matters to consider. If I were sued for malpractice, they would be liable, too. They were just protecting our patients, their practice, and ironically, me.

I promised to give them weekly urine examinations. If any mood-altering drugs were found in my urine, I would resign.

The urine tests came back clean week after week. My partners complimented me on my control. "Keep up the good work," they said.

After several weeks, however, my drug-addict thinking reemerged. They only took urine samples on Fridays. The drugs would show up in urine at least forty-eight hours after ingestion. I could drug-binge on the weekends and be clean by Friday. Who would know?

The following Monday I was asked to produce a urine specimen. "I won't be here this Friday," my partner said. "Let's get one today."

My heart raced. I was trapped. The primal instinct of fight or flight bombarded my senses. The drugs were still in my urine. Was there a way out?

"I don't think I can go right now. I'll drink some coffee. Give me about an hour."

Sixty minutes to consider the alternatives. I could resign and escape the embarrassment of failing again. (*What would you do? You have no idea of how to set up your own practice. Your practice is virtually gone anyway. How would you live?*) I could tell the truth and hope they would give me another chance. (*Would you? How many chances do you want?*) I could give them a urine and hope it comes back clean. (*Fat chance! Get serious!*) I could substitute a clean specimen for my own. (*I knew you'd come to that. Why not? You've lied and cheated before. What's one more time?*)

Where would I get a clean urine? A patient? Impossible. My nurses knew about the urine tests. They would know why

I wanted a patient's urine. A resident at the hospital? The residents, too, would find my request for their urine a little bizarre. And what if *they* were taking drugs?

I remembered the labor-and-delivery suite at Baylor Hospital. There were always pregnant patients' urine specimens on the counter waiting for the lab to collect them. I would simply steal a patient's urine—they could always get another. And pregnant patients don't use drugs. It was guaranteed to be clean.

The urine counter was empty. "The lab just came, Dr. Gehring," the ward secretary said. "If you need to check a specimen yourself, they're down at the lab. Do you have a patient—"

"Never mind," I said. I sat at the end of the counter and struck up a conversation with another doctor who had a patient in labor. "Do you have a patient here?" he asked. "No, just resting before I go back to the office," I replied. Still no specimen on the counter. My hour was almost up.

Finally a nurse placed a sample on the counter. I waited until the ward secretary left for coffee, and then walked to the counter, hid the container in my lab-coat pocket, and walked out the door.

My partner and I went to the lavatory for our weekly ritual. I closed the door of the stall and transferred the specimen into his container. I felt like garbage.

Two days later he came into my office. "They found Valium in your urine," he said.

Was the whole world on drugs? Even pregnant women? "Impossible!" I was indignant. "I haven't taken Valium in months. Must be a lab error."

"I suppose it could be." He paused, searching to make eye contact. Finding none, he sighed. "Yes, I suppose it could be. In fact, that's the only likely explanation, because the test also showed that you're pregnant." He didn't smile as he silently left my office.

Several days later I told both my partners the truth. They

gave me another chance. "We're thinking of your family, Bob," they said. "They deserve another chance."

Two months later I resigned. I was using drugs daily— there was no way of avoiding a dirty urine. My partners agreed to cover my practice "until I got well and could set up my own office." I thanked them and admitted myself to the Disabled Doctors Program in Atlanta, Georgia.

When I woke up in that small hospital in Atlanta, I was again withdrawing from massive doses of Dilaudid. This was my fourth hospitalization in less than a year. The Disabled Doctors Program required a minimum of four months hospitalization. Normal people stayed only one; doctors, four. It took at least that long to break through our egos. The classic axiom of "you can always tell a doctor, but you can't tell him much," applied.

The program in Atlanta taught me about honesty. They talked about "segmental honesty." I couldn't get well unless I was honest in all aspects of my life. The drug addiction was only one segment. If I ignored the other segments, I would use drugs again.

Three months into the program, I was arrested in downtown Atlanta for solicitation of a prostitute. The prostitute was an undercover policewoman. Six of her male colleagues wrestled me to the ground and announced, "We're from the Atlanta police, and you're under arrest."

They marched me down a dark street, hands pinned behind me. My only thought was that they were muggers— they were going to kill me for my money. The girl was just part of a rip-off scheme. "If y'all are police, please show me some identification." There was no concealing the fear in my voice. They produced their I.D.'s, and I remember saying, "Oh, thank God. You *are* police." They were astonished.

I was thrown into a drunk tank with at least fifty other guys. There was no ventilation, and the heat and humidity of a summer night in Georgia had us wringing wet in minutes. There were no benches; we sat on a concrete floor that sloped to a large drain in the center. An overflowing toilet sat in the corner. The other men vomited, urinated, and defecated on themselves. The smell was nauseating—I couldn't breathe.

I banged on the door. "Please let me out of here!" I screamed. "I don't belong here. Can't you understand? I'm a medical doctor, and I need to get out of here."

"Get away from that door, punk!" a burly guard replied. "You'll get out of the tank as soon as we get you processed."

"But you don't understand. I'm a doctor."

"Sure you are, man. And I'm Prince Phillip. Now get away from the door."

I produced my identification and begged the guard to process me soon. Flaunting that M.D. had worked so many times before, surely it would work now.

He looked at my I.D. "So you are a doctor. You know, I guess we're all doctors in a way. We all deal with human frailties and weaknesses. You deal with diseases of the body; I deal with diseases of the—"

"I don't want a philosophical discussion of our roles in society. I want to get out of here. You don't know how it feels to be locked in this hot room with these—"

"You'll get processed when you get processed. Consider it kinda like waiting in a waiting room. When it's your time, I'll just say 'the doctor will see you now, Doctor.'" His laugh was shrill and demeaning. "See how it feels to wait, Doctor."

I spent the night in the drunk tank staring at the walls, trying to keep from vomiting. Around 10:00 A.M. they fingerprinted me and took mug shots. Then I was taken upstairs and locked in a cell with three other men. I was scared.

"How do I get outa here?" I asked a cellmate.

"Didn't they let you make a phone call? You shoulda called your bondsman." He said it like *everyone* had a bondsman.

The guard finally unlocked the cell and led me to the telephone room. I called a bondsman, and he reluctantly agreed to post bail, though he wasn't too excited about accepting an out-of-town check for his services.

Sitting in that cell, I had plenty of time for reflection. I still couldn't believe the terrible things that were happening to me. Now I was a junkie doctor incarcerated on a morals charge. I felt like the principle character in somebody else's bad dream. Where was the strong farm boy who ran through plowed fields to condition himself for football? Where was that determined student who studied hard to get his doctorate in medicine? Where was that sensitive intern who cried over his patients? That same man couldn't be sitting in a jail in Atlanta, Georgia?

I remembered reading newspaper articles about men— intelligent men from good families—who just didn't fit into society. No matter how hard they tried, they continually committed one colossal screw-up after another. At times they meant well, but circumstances soon overwhelmed them—their end was always tragic. In fact, they seemed to self-sabotage their best efforts. Bad karma, I guess. I was one of those men—I would be another statistic in a newspaper.

I had lost the true respect of my family—they tolerated me. Why, I didn't know. I had lost my patients; I had lost my practice. Now I knew they would demand that I leave the rehabilitation program. I knew I would use drugs again. I knew I would die. It was just a matter of time.

Soon after my release from jail, I was asked to leave the Disabled Doctors Program. They talked about my segmental dishonesty. "Sure, you're honest about the drugs, but all other aspects of your life are still deranged. You can't be sexually dishonest and expect to recover from drug addiction. It just doesn't work—you need to change your whole life."

I was told my "defeatist attitude" was detrimental to the other doctors who seriously wanted to recover. "We can work with almost all the doctors who come into this program. A few, however, have a character defect that makes recovery virtually impossible. We can't waste our time with those individuals. We have too many others that deserve our attention." The chairman of the program sent me home with these final words: "You're dying, Bob. God help you."

Carolyn vividly remembers that summer of 1980. "I was alone in Dallas with three children and little money. We had already spent $22,000 on psychiatrists and hospitals. We needed money to set up Bob's new office. I still thought he'd recover and his patients would come back to him. But I knew I'd have to organize the office myself—he had no business sense at all.

"Our savings were gone, and I was borrowing money. Then Bob called and told me that he just got out of jail and needed money to pay his fine and the bondsman. Of course, my initial thought was that he had been arrested on some drug charge, but then he told me about the prostitute. I was shocked and very angry, to say the least. I knew about his dealings with prostitutes before we were married, but I couldn't believe he would do such a thing now. I was back here trying to keep the family together and make ends meet. He was down in Atlanta spending money on hookers when he was supposed to be getting well. He didn't even have the brains to know the difference between a hooker and a policewoman.

"He wanted me to come to Atlanta to be with him. 'What shall I use for money?' I asked. He didn't seem to understand that we were broke. He cried and begged. He told me he was afraid they'd kick him out of the program. For the first time in our marriage, I said 'no' to him. I told him that I would be supportive of his efforts to fight his addiction, but I couldn't tolerate his infidelity. This time he was on his own.

"I took the kids and stayed at a friend's chalet in Red River, New Mexico. I needed to get away—I needed to make some important decisions.

"My family had told me to leave Bob. Later, Bob's

brothers advised me to leave him. Even Bob told me to leave, especially after coming back from Atlanta.

"I was frustrated and exhausted. I guess if all those catastrophic things had happened at once, I would have divorced him. But the sequence of disastrous events happened so slowly and gradually, that there was always a glimmer of hope to keep me plugging. I was a fixer—certainly this whole thing could be fixed.

"During that week in Red River, I thought seriously of leaving him. Sure, I was afraid of the unknown, but anything was better than this constant madness. Drugs, hospitals, hookers—what was next? Was there no end to this tragedy?

"But when it came down to actually making a decision, I knew I could never leave him. Not while there was the slightest chance he could get well. I suppose I thought that I somehow contributed to his drug addiction. If only I could be this or that, then maybe he could stop the drugs. I was a typical 'spouse-aholic.'

"Had he been mean or violent, I would have left him in a second. But he wasn't. When he was normal, he was kind, gentle, and loving. When he was drugged, he was passive. But never violent. He never hurt me or the kids—not physically—and I knew he wouldn't.

"Of course he wasn't much of a father to the kids. Courtney, yes. She was his pride and joy. He doted on her. But he ignored the other children. Oh, he gave them everything they needed, but he always considered himself an outsider with them. He would say 'they're your kids.'

"And he was always so terribly sorry. Really sorry. He wasn't trying to con me—he was genuinely sorry for his behavior. His drug-addiction years were marked by his impulsive behavior. Even the hooker incident was impulsive—he never thought of the consequences. When he did, he was truly sorry. He was sick, and I accepted that. And I knew his remorse was sincere.

"But here was the crux. I loved Bob, and I knew he loved me. He was my best friend. How could I leave my best friend when he was in so much pain? So pitiful. He was addicted to drugs, and I was addicted to him. I knew I would never leave him, and I thought he would never leave me. So I hung onto the good memories of the old Bob, and I prayed for the good times to return. But I was no competition for his first love—his drugs.

"His return from Atlanta was disastrous. I had seen the look of defeat before, but never the total resignation he showed then. He again begged me to leave. 'I've lost my practice, my job, and our money,' he said. 'Let me paint the scenario—we'll set up the new office. Do you honestly think any patients will come to me? I'll lose that, too. I'll eventually lose my license. I'll start buying drugs off the street, and if I'm not killed in a car accident, I'll kill myself. Please take the kids and make a life for them. You don't deserve the humiliation that I will bring on us. My life is over. You don't need to die with me.'

"He made several token efforts to recover during those months after Atlanta. He went to a hypnotist who had office hours starting at 4:00 A.M. 'If that's too early, I'll just call you on the phone and hypnotize you. The fee is the same.' Bob saw him at 5:00 A.M. several times at his office; then he called and hypnotized Bob at home. Bob felt that he was a poor hypnotic subject, which I'm sure was true, and he finally gave up the idea entirely.

"He also saw an aversion therapist who wired him to electricity and shocked him while showing him pictures of drugs and syringes. He stopped seeing him, too. 'Even death itself doesn't deter me from drugs. Do you think an electric shock will?'

"Finally, he enrolled in a government-sponsored methadone program. All of the clients were heroin addicts who were now addicted to the methadone dispensed weekly by the clinic for a paltry sum of fifteen dollars. I felt so sorry for him—he'd stand in line with the pimps, pushers, hookers, and felons of Dallas to get his daily dose of methadone. 'I don't look down on those people, Carolyn,' he told me.

'They're doing better than I am. They'll be alive long after I'm dead!'

"The methadone was supposed to help him keep off the other drugs. They checked his urine weekly and each week found drugs other than methadone. They warned him repeatedly to no avail. 'They'll kick me out soon,' he said. 'Either that or the medical examiners will find out—it won't be long.'

"They once reprimanded him for his continual drug binges and proceeded to read a list of drugs they found in his urine. Morphine, codeine, cocaine, . . . the list went on and on. Bob nodded his head with each drug. 'Darvon, Seconal, Demerol, heroin—' 'Just a darned minute,' Bob interrupted. He was indignant. 'I have never used heroin.' He was still fighting for some vestige of honor.

"After Atlanta he made no attempt to conceal his drug addiction. The only exception was at the hospital. He never went to the hospital loaded—in fact, he seldom went to the hospital. He had no patients.

"He still had the key to his old office, and he began to steal drugs from his ex-partners. He would wait until the office staff left for the evening, withdraw several cc.'s of Demerol from the bottle and replace it with sterile water so that the theft wouldn't be noticed. He later told them the truth. They replaced the bottle of Demerol with a new one and asked for his office key. That night he had the security guard open the office, and he stole the new bottle.

"He was never without an ample supply of drugs. He'd put the loaded syringes in his socks so that he'd have them wherever he went. They had needle guards on them, so he wouldn't stick himself. He would excuse himself and go to the bathroom to shoot up.

"Frequently he'd call and ask me to come and drive him home. I would usually find him in his office, passed out on the floor. If he could drive, he'd come home with blood stains on his sleeves and vomit on his shirt.

"That's what I couldn't understand. At times the drugs

would make him so terribly sick that he'd retch and retch. When he finally did stop vomiting, he'd inject some more drugs and start all over again.

"Why didn't I call the doctors in his group and get him back in the hospital? I threatened many times. He'd simply laugh and say, 'There's not a hospital in the country that would accept me. Are you kidding? I've been kicked out of the best. Your only recourse is a state insane asylum and I can assure you, I'll never be incarcerated again. But that's your decision.' It was the old rock-and-hard-place thing. He was killing himself, but if I called someone, he'd kill himself.

"The breaking point finally came, however. Late one night when all the kids were asleep, I heard Bob's voice in the kitchen. There was no one else in the house. Who was he talking to? I stood outside the kitchen door and listened. He was hallucinating incoherently, but I caught certain distinct phrases. 'Get that blood going. She's dying—she's dying and I can't stop the bleeding. Help her, somebody help her. . . .'

"I was frightened and started crying. Then he saw me and seemed to snap out of his delirium. Seeing the fear in my face, he started to apologize. I asked if he knew what he had done. He replied that he assumed he was dreaming. He said he dreamed that he was delivering a baby and his patient kept bleeding and bleeding and he couldn't stop it. 'Do you know where you are?' Yes, in the kitchen. 'Were you asleep?' No, he was wide awake. 'Do normal people dream when they're wide awake, standing in the kitchen?' He didn't answer.

"The years of frustration erupted. 'Look at you, Bob. Just look at you. I've never been afraid of you before, but now I'm scared to death. You don't know what you're doing anymore. Your brain is so scrambled by those drugs that I'm afraid for me and the kids. I can't take it. I'm losing my mind *with* you. I need help. If you won't get help, so be it. But I can't live like this.'

"He left that night. He was so drugged that I feared for

his life. When he didn't return, I bundled Courtney up and went looking for him. He was asleep on the floor of his office. I begged him to come home, but he said that he wouldn't. He said that he wouldn't humiliate me or the kids any longer. He was going to live in his office until the State Board revoked his license. He warned me that if I called anyone, he would blow his brains out. 'I don't think you want that on your conscience,' he said. I asked what was going to happen after the board revoked his license. He didn't answer.

"In the following weeks I called him daily. He never returned my calls; I knew he wouldn't. But at least I could call the answering service to see if he'd picked up my messages. Then I'd know he was still alive.

"Occasionally he came home to get more clothes and to see Courtney. When he did, he always started an argument, as though he needed to justify his separation from us. But we both knew that anger wasn't the divisive factor—drugs were.

"On Thanksgiving day, 1980, Bob showed up for dinner completely spaced out on cocaine. We were all at my mom's. My family tried to be congenial, but Bob just sat and stared out the window. He didn't eat; he didn't talk; he just stared. After a short time, he left without even saying good-by.

"The next time I saw him was on December 7th. He came home very late and spent almost an hour talking to Courtney. Courtney was asleep the whole time. At only twenty-one months, she couldn't have understood him anyway. But I heard him talking and crying. He came into our bedroom after leaving Courtney. I said something like, 'It's good to see you again.' He didn't speak. He just buried his head on my shoulder and cried. Finally, he left. He hadn't spoken a word to me.

"I prayed so hard that night."

THE FINAL BATTLE

Cocaine, Nitrous Oxide, Sodium Pentothal

"I want out."

Pardon me for laughing, Doctor. But I don't do business that way. A deal's a deal.

"But I'm dying. Don't you care?"

Not a bit. You were born to die. You know that.

"But I'm only thirty-eight. I've got a family."

You had a family. Look, friend, I can't help you. Don't even want to. Dying? You've been dead for years. I can't change that. But you can go out in style. And I do mean style.

"What are you talking about?"

Let's go to the elixir department. . . .

"No! No elixirs. No drugs."

I'm surprised you haven't thought of this elixir on your own. After all, with all your status. It's a status elixir. Only the beautiful people can afford it. Movie stars, pro athletes, doctors. And get this, it's nonaddicting. Can you believe it?

"Don't lie to me. I knew patients in the drug hospitals who spent millions on that drug. They sold their souls to the devil for cocaine. . . ."

Pardon my laughter, friend. Look who's talking about soul-selling. But seriously, now, think about it. Did any of your hospital friends complain of physical pain when they stopped taking cocaine?

"No, but they went into suicidal depression. Which is

worse? Psychologically it's the most addicting drug known to medicine."

I just can't understand you. Years ago you wanted an elixir to enhance sex. Now I'm offering you sex, pure sex, in the form of a white powder, and you're turning it down.

"Can't you understand? I'm dying! And you're talking about cocaine."

Get serious, stupid. That's the whole point. You're dead. What difference does it make? The whole world knows you're a junkie. At the most, I'd give you a month to live anyway. Go out in style, man.

I bought the cocaine from pushers. I knew I couldn't write a prescription for it—there were few medical uses for cocaine, and a gynecologist certainly wouldn't use it in his practice. It costs over one hundred dollars a gram. I bought it with the money Carolyn had borrowed.

In *Man's Search for Meaning,* Victor Frankl related his observations of men dying in a concentration camp. Cigarettes were used as barter by the inmates of the death camp. Frankl said he could always tell when a man resigned himself to his inevitable death—the man began smoking his cigarettes instead of spending them. I was smoking my last cigarettes.

Cocaine is the ultimate high, and I was using it suicidally. I'd mix the cocaine with water and never even bother to measure the dosage. After injection, I knew I'd either be drugged or dead—the outcome really didn't matter.

Cocaine is also the ultimate low. When you stop using it, you immediately have a psychic pain worse than any physical pain imaginable. People kill themselves rather than experience that feeling. It eventually subsides (after four or five hours), but during its peak, your whole being is in the throes of indescribable mental anguish. The depression is literally suicidal.

In the midst of the psychic pain after one cocaine binge,

I remembered a tank of nitrous oxide that I used for cryosurgery. I can't say that I consciously wanted to die at that time—I just wanted to stop the post-cocaine depression. I placed the nitrous tank on the floor and opened the valve. I heard the hiss of the gas as it escaped the container. I lay beside the tank and pressed my mouth over the metal outlet. The gas filled my lungs quickly, and I felt the pain lessen. Soon I was sleepy, and the pain was completely gone.

I remembered that nitrous tanks would freeze up when I used them for cryosurgery. I felt the metal on my lips get colder and colder. But it didn't hurt, and I knew if I stopped breathing that gas, the pain would come back.

The hissing of the gas was the only sound I heard—it seemed miles away. I felt like I was in a large wooden barrel and someone was slowly beating on it with a large hammer. I finally realized that the noise was my own heartbeat, and I began getting frightened. I tried pulling my lips from the tank, but they wouldn't budge. They were frozen solid against the metal.

I struggled to extricate myself from the source of that lethal gas. I felt the skin from my lips pull off, but I couldn't free myself completely. My muscles were getting weaker, my struggling less intense. My lips were bleeding and I saw frozen blood on the tank. The hammer sound went away; now I could only hear the sound of my breathing—getting shorter and farther apart. I was still conscious and can remember thinking "So this is death. So this is what all men fear." I didn't fear it. Whether it was the effects of the nitrous oxide or lack of oxygen to my brain or what all humans sense when they die, I don't know. I only know I welcomed death.

I can remember my last breath. I was waiting for the next one, but it never came. There were soft white lights— brilliant lights that weren't harsh at all, but very pleasant. Music seemed to come from within me. Music like I had never heard before. Beautiful music.

I thought of Mr. Peterson and knew I was dying. But I also remember explaining this sensation, even while it was happening, as anoxia. I am hallucinating because my brain is deprived of oxygen, I reasoned. I'm dying, but I'm certainly not dead.

I entered a long, white corridor.

When I awoke, it was morning. I was lying beside the tank. My lips were free, though throbbing in pain. Blood stained the carpet. I couldn't believe it—I was alive.

The tank was empty. It must have been almost empty when I passed out. I was still alive because the tank ran out of gas!

Sunday, December 7, 1980. Thirty-nine years earlier, Admiral Yamamoto had unleashed the destructive power of the Japanese Empire on Pearl Harbor and started a war. Now, thirty-nine years later, General Gehring unleashed the destructive power of the demons within him and ended a war.

All good generals know the strength and deployment of their enemy. They never fight on against insurmountable odds. They surrender and life goes on.

In my battle against addiction, I hadn't won so much as a skirmish. I was surrounded, outmanned, outmaneuvered, overpowered. How many times, after losing a decisive battle, had I faced my enemy with a sincere resolve and announced, "I will beat you on will power alone"? How many times did "General Drug Addiction" laugh in my face and then annihilate me in another humiliating battle?

But that was over now. Like all good generals, I was ready to surrender to a superior force. But, unlike the great soldiers I admired, I could not announce "death before dishonor." No, the dishonor preceded my death by years.

That morning I awoke on the floor of my office and cleaned up the syringes from the night before. The office Muzak was already playing Christmas carols. "Joy to the World." I almost laughed.

I remembered Sunday mornings at home in North Dakota. Dad would throw his grease-stained farmer overalls in the clothes hamper and don his only suit. "Sunday's not Sunday unless I wear a suit," he would say. "It shows respect for God when we dress up on His day." Mom would put a pot roast in the oven, and we'd all go to church. The world *was* joyful then. But that was a thousand years ago.

I called my parents. I knew it would be our last conversation. They knew nothing of my drug addiction— they were a thousand miles away. I wished them a Merry Christmas and told them to cancel their plans to visit us. Yes, I had left Carolyn, and we were getting a divorce. No, nothing else was wrong. Things would work out. I love you, too. Good-by. I hung up before the tears came.

Church bells were ringing when I called my pusher. "Can you front me two more grams?"

"Front you? Are you kidding? You already owe me three hundred dollars."

"You don't understand. I need it badly."

"Sure, Doctor. Don't we all? But *you* don't seem to understand that I'm a businessman. You're hooked, man. Cocaine is your staple. Does your grocery store front you when you buy potatoes?"

I was begging. "Can't we make some kind of deal? I need it. It's my life. . . ."

"You junkies scare me. You're a doctor, man. You're begging like a baby. I'd like to do business with you, but I think you need help. Get yourself back to recreational use, and I'll talk to you—"

"Wait! I've got a watch. I'll give you my watch."

"Rolex?"

"Seiko."

Laughter. "Come on, Doc. Get serious. We're talking five hundred dollars. The three that you owe me plus two more. A Seiko just won't cut it."

"My coin collection. I've got a coin collection. You can have it."

"Silver dollars?"

"A bunch—some very rare ones. Please."

"Bring it over, and we'll talk."

I had been saving that collection for my kids. It was worth three times what he gave me, but I had my cocaine. Joy to the world.

I finished my binge late that night, then waited for the depression. It came with an unparalleled magnitude. Even death was better.

I drove home and went into Courtney's room. She was asleep, so innocent and precious. I wept.

"Courtney, I've waited so long for you. Even when you were in Mommy's tummy, I dreamed of you. I felt you kick. I heard your little heart beating. I loved you even then.

"When you were born, I had great plans for you—for us. I wanted to give you a life of happiness. Not success, but happiness. But I guess that's what success is, isn't it? I hope you find it, but you'll have to find it without me for I'm going to leave you.

"You'll have a daddy, and I'm sure he'll give you a better life than I could have given you. Your mom will marry again. I just hope your stepfather will treat you better than I treated your brother and sister. Be good to him in return.

"There is money set aside for you. Insurance money. You'll get a good education and have children of your own and—"

My tears were dripping on her pretty little face. I dried them as best I could.

"You're the crowning achievement of my life. You're the best thing I've ever done. All that status, that M.D., that money was nothing in comparison to you, Courtney. I love you so much.

"When you get older, someone will tell you that your daddy was addicted to drugs. They'll tell you that your daddy committed suicide. I don't expect you to understand. You won't even remember me. But I hope your mother tells you that I loved you, that I was a good person who couldn't find a way out. Please forgive me. Oh, please, please forgive me. I'm so terribly sorry."

I cradled that innocent child in my arms and rocked her back and forth. I couldn't put her down. She slept in spite of my hysterical sobbing. "I'm sorry, honey. I'm so sorry." I must have repeated my apology at least fifty times. Finally, I laid her back in her bed and said good-by.

Then I went into Carolyn's room. She was awake and said something to me. I hugged her for a long time. No words, just tears that never stopped.

As I drove the twenty-five miles to the hospital, I remembered the stock questions asked of me in every rehabilitation hospital I had been in: "Have you thought about suicide?" The radio was playing Kenny Roger's "You've got to know when to hold 'em; know when to fold 'em." How appropriate. I was holding a losing hand; it was time to fold it.

I thought about writing a note. Wasn't that the protocol for suicide? What would I say? That life wasn't worth living? That the drugs had finally won? What an insulting redundancy—my whole life was a suicide note. I didn't need to explain my death.

Did I think about heaven or hell? The life after? Yes, but only in an abstract way. I was scared, to be sure, but if it did exist, could hell be worse than this?

"Have you planned your suicide?" Potassium chloride was my first choice. It was foolproof. Your heart just stopped. Painless. But where would I get potassium chloride at this time of night? It was well past midnight, and most pharmacies were closed. The hospital pharmacy was open all night, but the pharmacists there all knew I was a drug addict. They wouldn't give me an aspirin.

I knew Sodium Pentothal was always available on the anesthesia carts in the operating rooms or delivery rooms of the hospital. Pentothal is a powerful anesthetic. It induced sleep and, in higher doses, death. But what dosage? It didn't matter. I'd just steal a bunch of it and inject it all. Painless. Sleep. Death. Freedom.

I entered the labor-and-delivery suite and put on my scrubs. I couldn't enter the delivery rooms in street clothes. It was a slow night. The nurses were all sitting at the front having coffee. The cleaning crew was in the back with nothing to do. They had full view of the delivery rooms; I couldn't get by them without arousing suspicion.

I took the elevator to the fifth-floor surgical suite. It was empty. I was about to enter an operating room when a nurse appeared from nowhere.

"Dr. Gehring! Dr. Gehring, what are you doing here?"

"Ah . . . I was told Dr. Anderson had a . . . ah . . . case up here. I was just looking for him."

She cocked her head in disbelief. "Dr. Anderson hasn't been here all night, and no cases are scheduled. Why don't you just be a good boy and go home and get some sleep. Looks like you could use some." Patronizing. Condescending. How else do you talk to a pitiful junkie?

The cleaning crew was gone when I got back down to Labor and Delivery. The Pentothal was in my pocket in a second, and I headed for the call room. The door had no lock, so I propped a chair against it. I was shaking in fear.

I withdrew the anesthetic from the larger container and filled a syringe, then filled a second syringe in case the first was not enough. I wished I knew exactly the lethal dose. What if I didn't kill myself? What if I rendered myself a vegetable and didn't die? I filled a third syringe.

The veins in my arms were scarred and useless, especially after that day's consumption of two grams of cocaine. I would have to use the femoral vein.

The femoral vein and artery are two large-caliber blood vessels that supply the leg. They lie directly beside each other in the groin. I would have to be certain to hit the vein rather than the artery. They weren't visible; it would be a blind stick.

I felt for the femoral pulse. It was strong. Was the vein

medial or lateral to the artery? I couldn't remember. No matter, I would find it.

I injected the drug quickly and felt a searing pain in my leg. I had hit the artery. I reflexively pulled back and a geyser of blood shot from the bounding vessel. All the better—if the drug didn't kill me, that bleeding artery would. I quickly found the vein and began to empty the syringe. I remembered the anesthesiologists telling patients to expect a garlic taste in their mouths before they went to sleep. I tasted it and thought "garlic—what a fitting end to a tasteless life."

The general had surrendered to the enemy. The war was over.

TRUE SURRENDER

I opened my eyes and tried to focus on a blurred figure in the background. I tried to get up but fell backward. My leg was throbbing. "Don't move," the apparition said. "You've lost a lot of blood. I'll get you some coffee."

Was I hallucinating again? This was my office, not the call room. How did I get here? I remembered waking up in the call room, lying in a pool of blood, and injecting more Pentothal. More garlic—more blackness. Why wasn't I dead? Had I botched that, too?

When he helped me sit up, I finally recognized the figure as Dr. Jim Boyd. "Careful, it's hot," he said.

I took the cup from his hand. It *was* hot. I wasn't hallucinating. I was still alive. And even in my semianesthetized state, I was not surprised that the person helping me was Jim Boyd.

Jim Boyd was an enviable doctor. He was a man who had combined his excellent technical skills with an ethical, Christian approach to the practice of medicine. It was a combination that made him respected and admired by both colleagues and patients and had earned him one of the largest OB-Gyn practices in Dallas.

But Jim was more than a good doctor. Always soft-spoken, humble, dependable, and diplomatic, he had risen quickly in the political hierarchy of Dallas's medical community. His tactful altruism served as a useful buffer between the diverse factions of the ego-inflated men of medicine. He was an officer of the Dallas County Medical Society and was on the advisory board of the OB-Gyn department of Baylor Hospital. He was a powerful man.

Jim and I had been friends years ago when I was an intern. He had taught me much of what I knew about OB-Gyn. But slowly, as our lifestyles grew more divergent, our friendship waned. It seemed that the higher he rose, the lower I sank.

But I knew why he was here now, and I knew our old friendship could not stay the inevitable. I feared his power, for I knew he had come to revoke my hospital privileges— and license. The ultimate humiliation.

"I want to help you, Bob," he said. "I saw the blood in the call room. I know about the Pentothal. I can't stand back and watch you kill yourself any longer."

My mind was playing tricks again. Help me? Sure, he wants to help me into a padded cell so I won't kill myself. I had attempted suicide in *his* hospital. He was merely a spokesman for the powers-that-be: "Get rid of him, Jim. We can't tolerate a suicidal junkie on our staff. Lock him up before he hurts someone."

"What happened last night?" Jim continued.

"I . . . ah . . . just went on another drug binge, Jim. That's all."

"With Pentothal, Bob? We both know that Pentothal is an anesthetic. It knocks you out and eventually kills you. I know you weren't taking it to get high."

"Sleep, Jim. I just wanted to sleep. I'm sorry. I can't think too well. I'm still a little groggy."

"Why all the blood? The mattress was soaked."

"I made a mistake and hit an artery. That's all. Honest."

Jim sensed the reason for my reticence. "Bob, I'm not here in any official capacity. Whether you wanted to or not, you almost died last night. You've been dying for years. I can't, with a clear conscience, allow your death to continue, because I firmly believe you don't want to die. I don't know what plan God has for you. I just know that He doesn't want you to die with a needle in your arm. I knew you before the drugs, Bob. I saw you cry when your puppy died. I'm here as your friend; I sincerely want to help you. Nothing you tell me will ever leave this office; you have my word on that. I'm on your side."

I started crying again. "You remember the puppy?"

Years earlier, Jim and I had been in the TV room at the hospital awaiting a delivery when the vet called and notified me of my puppy's death. Jim had known by our conversation that something bad had happened. I had tried to camouflage my grief; after all, it was only a puppy. But the tears had come anyway. He had remembered that!

"Of course, I remember. Anybody who cries over the death of a puppy can't be all bad. There is good in you, Bob. And where there is good, there is God. Let's see if we can find that God, together."

"You're not going to revoke my hospital privileges?"

He laughed, his true Christian humility surfacing. "You overestimate my importance. I couldn't revoke your privileges even if I wanted to. However, I can't guarantee that the hospital won't ask for your resignation, especially after last night. I'll do everything in my power to keep you on the staff, but only under certain conditions. Fair enough?"

I agreed, but only out of respect for Jim Boyd. He was going out on a limb for me; I couldn't say no to his conditions. And his only condition that day was that I not use drugs until he saw me again that evening. I hoped I could keep this promise.

Jim said a prayer for me and departed with the promise that he'd return to my office at 5:30 that evening. Ironically, I felt sorry for him. My drug addiction would destroy his best efforts. He was going to bat for me, and I was sure I'd embarrass him. If I couldn't give up the needle for Courtney or Carolyn or my medical practice—if death itself was no deterrent, what could Jim Boyd offer?

I knew he'd offer me his faith in Jesus Christ. But that's exactly what it would be. His faith, not mine. After my inevitable failure, what about him? The God who was so powerful in his life would fail in mine. My failure would be his failure, too, and Jim Boyd didn't fail in anything he set his mind to. Would *our* failure destroy his faith in God? I hoped that it wouldn't. I had dragged many innocent people into the depths of my despair. I didn't want to do that to Jim Boyd, too.

I sensed his concern and compassion. He seemed to understand. But how could he? He was a Christian. Surely a man like him could not comprehend a life so intolerable that drug addiction was the only recourse.

He said he couldn't stand by and watch me die. How would he prevent it? An asylum? A padded cell? Anything short of that would be futile.

But he had offered to help. Without monetary compensation, without any advantage to him that I could perceive. What were his motives? Certainly Christian love didn't extend this far. He'd soon give up. You can't give life to a dead man.

"Do you know what you're getting into?" I asked him that evening. "I've been in four hospitals. They kicked me out of the mecca of drug rehabilitation centers in Atlanta for solicitation of a prostitute and a bad attitude. I've been addicted to almost every drug known to medical science. I admire your willingness to help—but it's hopeless. Absolutely hopeless. As a friend, I can't accept your help when I feel that your efforts will fail. I have to be honest."

I expected him to write me off then and there. He simply smiled. "There is nothing hopeless to the power of Jesus Christ," he said. "And yes, I know your history. All that's in the past. You're not going to believe the person you will become in a very short time. You need another addiction. A positive addiction. Christ is *the* positive addiction."

Silence. Then, "Jim," I began. I wanted to change the subject. I had heard this argument so many times before. "I really—"

"I'm sorry, Bob. I know what you're going to say. I guess I'm ignoring the basics. Do you believe in God?"

"Yes, sir." He laughed when I gave him my explanation of the Cosmic Scientist.

"He's certainly that, to be sure. But He's so much more. Do you believe in Jesus Christ?"

I didn't want to alienate this good man, but I had to be truthful. "I believe Christ was a great man," I answered.

"You don't believe Christ is the Son of God?"

"No, sir."*(I can't believe a great cosmic God would play a cheap trick like sending his son to be exterminated by madmen. Just because he taught love? Not a chance. Any God that can create quasars or DNA surely would have a better plan than that.)* "Jim, I believe Christ was a great man. But like all the great men of his time, Alexander the Great and the Caesars, he soon became engulfed in his own messianic complex. Granted, he was convincing. Lesser men, namely biographers, like to shroud their leaders in myth and legend. Christ was no exception." Again I expected him to walk out the door.

Instead he smiled and said, "Well, I guess we have a lot to work on, don't we? But that's the beauty of it all. You don't *have* to believe in the divinity of Christ initially. You just have to read His word and follow His teachings, and something divine, something supernatural happens to you. You can't explain that 'something' in human terms. Then, there can be no other explanation than Christ's divinity. It happened to me; it will happen to you, too. But at this point, the divinity of Christ is academic. You're dying. What you need is a design for living, and Christ can give you that."

"Yes, sir." Where did he get his confidence, his optimism?

"I noticed that the great men you cited were military leaders. You like military history?"

"Yes, sir. Alexander the Great, Julius Caesar, Erwin Rommel—"

"Tell me, what lasting contribution did these men make? How did they influence your life?"

I paused to ponder his question. I had no good answer.

Jim leaned forward and continued. "Let's assume for the moment that Christ was only a man, as you say. But consider this. Christ never used a sword; He never had an army; His campaign lasted only three years. Yet this man, as you call Him, changed the course of history. Millions of lives for two millennia have been transformed because of Him. Can you honestly say that about any other person in history? What lasting contribution did Erwin Rommel make? Can you apply any aspect of Rommel's life to your own?"

I couldn't believe what I was hearing. For twenty years I had rejected Christianity because it was always presented with an are-you-saved twist of the arm. Now someone was telling me about Christ in terms I could understand. I knew the drugs had slowed the synapses of my brain, but Jim's words were clear and cogent. I listened.

"Bob," he continued, "I'm going to be absolutely frank with you. We doctors, myself included, get caught up in our pseudointellectualism. We like to take the credit when our patients get well. By the same token, we absorb the blame when our patients die. We play God. I found out a long time ago that we doctors are merely God's technicians. Doctors treat disease; only God can heal."

Again he had hit home. I knew the God complex; I had *lived* the God complex.

"So much for that for now. Did you use drugs today?"

"No, sir. But I thought about drugs all day. I was tempted every five minutes."

"Of course. I knew you would be tempted. But you didn't use any. You met the beginning step of condition number one.

"Next Monday you are to meet with the hospital administrators and the chairman of the OB-Gyn department. I don't know what their decision will be, but if you'd like, I'll go with you. You might need some moral support. I'll do all I can, *if* you follow my other conditions to the letter."

"Of course. What are they, Jim?"

"Number two. You *will* attend church with me every Sunday. Without fail. Agreed?"

"Yes, sir."

"And I will meet with you at 5:30 every day until you pull out of this. We're going to read the Bible; we're going to pray. Together. Soon you'll be reading and praying on your own, but initially I'll help you."

"You don't have time for that, Jim. I know the size of your practice."

"I'll make time. Number three. If you ever use drugs again, you will tell me, and we'll decide then whether or not you need to surrender your medical license. And along that line, I want you to check with me before you do any surgery, however minor. For the safety of your patients, the hospital, and yourself. You can understand that, I'm sure."

"The surgery is no problem. I have very few patients."

"You will have—your patients will start coming back, believe me." Again the optimism.

"And yes, I'll tell you about the drugs. I owe it to you to be honest."

"Good. Please understand, I'm not saying that you would lie to me, but I know that all drug addicts have a great capacity for deception. I may ask you for spot urine tests anytime I want to. . . . Finally, you will meet with Dan Griffin for spiritual counseling. Do you agree to those conditions?"

What could I say? "Yes, sir. I will do anything you ask. But please, tell me this will work. And keep telling me it will work, because right now I feel so hopeless. Everything else has failed—please tell me this will work."

"It will work, Bob. God's on our side. Believe me, it will work. Any questions?"

"Who's Dan Griffin?"

"Dan's the pastor of my church. You'll see him this Sunday."

(*A Baptist preacher. Oh, no. Hellfire and brimstone. Be washed in the blood of the lamb. Put your trust in Jee'zus. Are you saved? Have you accepted JEE'zus as your PERSON-AL-LORD-AND-SAVIOR? I've got a solution to your problem, son. Just stop taking them drugs. Jee'zus saves.*)

"Jim, I know I'm not in a position to negotiate, but I've talked to preachers before." I explained the reasons for my reluctance.

Jim laughed. "You'll like Dan," he said. "Let's say a prayer."

And so it began. The first step in that proverbial thousand-mile journey. I stopped taking drugs; I sweated the residual out of my system. But the anger, resentment, depression, and paranoia persisted for months afterward. I was irrational, irritable, and totally unrealistic.

"We arrived in Dallas on Monday, December 8," my brother Bill remembers. "Mom had called to tell me that Bob had left Carolyn and was getting a divorce. Our parents had to cancel their Christmas trip because of that. I immediately knew something catastrophic had happened—and I knew it was more than marital problems. I had known of my younger brother's addiction for many years. We had always been very close—he confided in me. But he had made me promise never to tell anyone else in the family. Especially Mom and Dad. The time for secrets was past. I called our brother Del, an OB-Gyn in Iowa. Gloria (my wife), Del, and I flew to Dallas to investigate.

"This person, . . . this ghost . . . met us at the airport. We could hardly recognize him. He could barely walk, he was limping so badly. I asked about his leg—he didn't answer. We stopped at his office, and I finally persuaded him to let me examine his leg. It was horrible. His whole right thigh was swollen and black and blue. Signs of a severe infection were already evident. He then tearfully admitted he had injected drugs into his femoral artery in an attempt to kill himself.

"As a doctor, I knew that as a result of the damage he had inflicted he could lose that leg from gangrene or infection. I told him he needed to be hospitalized.

"He exploded in rage. 'Now I know why you're here. You've come to commit me. My own brothers!' We had no intention of committing him. I wrote him a prescription for antibiotics and hoped for the best. He alternated between severe depression and anger, crying one moment and raging the next. During our whole stay, I sensed that he was paranoid about our committing him.

"Checking his appointment book in the office, I saw he had few, if any, patients. He was to meet with the hospital administration to determine his future at the hospital. I assumed he was being investigated by the state board. He had no money. He had depleted his life's savings and was living on money that Carolyn had borrowed. Yet he had gone out and bought $1,000 worth of office furniture for an office that probably would be closed in two weeks. He was totally irrational. I wanted to shake him.

"Del and I met with Jim Boyd and a physician from the Doctors Helping Doctors group to decide how we could help Bob. The doctor from the group wanted to send him to another hospital. I sensed that he didn't know what else to do with Bob. Neither did we, but we agreed with Jim that another hospitalization would just be a temporary effort. 'We're all doctors here,' Jim said. 'We all know that if a patient doesn't respond to one treatment regimen, there is no sense repeating it over and over. He needs to recover outside of a hospital environment. He needs to get well here in Dallas.' We were most impressed with Dr. Boyd.

"I was angry with Bob about the daily methadone. He said he was going to get off the drug, but by that time Bob had become the consummate con artist. I didn't know whether to believe him or not. We argued, and I bitterly called him a con man. I repeated it over and over in my anger. He finally left and drove to his office to spend the night. He was still sleeping on the floor there. Later he called to apologize for his anger.

"That's the paradox. There were so many times that I saw the old Bob in him—the kid brother I remembered so well. The good Bob. At other times, he was a total stranger— surly, uncommunicative, angry, and paranoid.

"We took Carolyn to dinner and told her to divorce him. We couldn't understand why she hadn't left long before. She told us that she still had hope. We could only admire her perseverance.

"Del, Gloria, and I flew home before Christmas. On the plane we talked about the brother we once had. The curly-haired, mischievous little imp whose antics had us in stitches most of our childhood. We talked about the tall, idealistic young medical student who had had so much going for him. It was gone now. We didn't know the man we had just visited in Dallas.

"We admired Jim Boyd for trying to help our brother, but we had a feeling that nothing would work for him. Nothing. Del expressed my thoughts succinctly. 'Bill, I have a gnawing feeling that the next time we see Bob will be at his funeral.' I tearfully agreed."

The following Sunday, and every Sunday thereafter, I went to church with Jim and Jan Boyd. As I listened to the organ music, I remembered some of the words to the more familiar hymns, especially "A Mighty Fortress is Our God." I needed that fortress.

I looked at the members of the congregation. Their faces reflected a peace and serenity that I hadn't seen for a long time and certainly not in the world I'd been existing in. They lived in the same jungle as I did; yet they were as content as I was miserable. The world wasn't killing them the way it was killing me. I wanted what they had.

I arranged my first meeting with Dan Griffin. Jim was right—I *did* like him. I couldn't believe he was a Baptist preacher. His presentation of Christianity was similar to Jim's—intelligent and palatable. We discussed the concept of the wounded healer—that true healing comes from weakness to weakness; not from strength to weakness. He told me that eventually my weakness would become my strength, and I would use it to help other people. At that time it made no sense at all, but Dan's personality was so overwhelming that I thought he must know what he was talking about. So I passively agreed with him.

Although both Dan and Jim were not much older than I, I related to them as father figures. Eventually, they became big brothers. Then, true friends. I grew to love them dearly.

But I kept waiting for this miraculous healing that they promised. Jim and I met daily for months—he even called me daily while he was on vacation. Dan and I met every Wednesday and Saturday. I had stopped taking drugs. Why wasn't I getting well?

I got discouraged. On three occasions I used drugs again. I gave up, but they didn't. "You didn't get addicted overnight; you won't recover overnight," they said. "Let's try again."

In my discouragement, Jim was always there with words of encouragement. "Bob, I think you're looking for a 'burning bush.' You want to win another door prize. That would be nice, but God may talk to you in a 'wee small voice.' Be patient."

Because of Jim's influence, the hospital didn't revoke my privileges. The state board never questioned me. My patients started to return.

I called Carolyn and begged her to take me back. She cried and said that she had been praying that I would return. I did—and never left again.

Months later I was reading the Bible to Jim as usual at one of our evening meetings. He always had me read, telling me to stop and discuss any passage that I found significant. I had read to him for months and never found anything worthy of discussion. Most of the time I read simply because he wanted me to read. Nothing was sinking in.

On this particular evening we were reading in Luke, and I read where Christ said, "The kingdom of God is within you." I read a few more words, then stopped. I went back to that passage and read it again. I looked up at Jim and repeated the passage. He was smiling.

"Is that the 'wee small voice' we're looking for, Bob?"

"Jim, that's a door prize! Is it really? Is the kingdom of God really within me? Has it been there all the time?"

"Of course it has, Bob. God never deserted you; you deserted him. He is all-powerful, Bob. And if God's power is within you, all you have to do is *tap* it. And He never runs out; the power is unlimited."

It seemed so simple—why had I overlooked it? I had spent thousands of dollars thinking the answer was in psychiatrists, hypnotists, aversion therapy, and hospitals. I had thought the great Cosmic Scientist was too powerful, too knowledgeable to care what happened to Bob Gehring. But if God were within me, then I, too, had the power and knowledge of the universe. I was a king because I had the kingdom of God.

"I'm going to get well," I said softly. "I know it now, Jim. I'm going to get well."

"I know it, too, Bob. I've always known it. Thank God."

"Bob used that Bible verse as his theme song," Carolyn remembers. "Sure he was tempted to use drugs. But he would say, 'No. Drugs are not a viable alternative. I have the power of God in me, and together we will resist this temptation.' And they did. He started getting well.

"I had prayed for Bob's recovery—God had answered my prayers. Bob was no longer taking drugs; he was gaining self-esteem and getting control of his own life. He was attending meetings and talking to other people with similar problems. He was making new friends and was busy in his recovery program.

"But as he got better, I got worse. It didn't make sense to me at the time, but later I realized what had happened. Other people seemed to be replacing me. I felt threatened. It was time for me to let go of the reins, but I held on tighter than ever. Also, I had grown accustomed to our pathological relationship. Bob's drug addiction had been so overwhelming that we hadn't had time to deal with anything else. As miserable as our life had been, it had been constant. Though constantly miserable, I had learned to live in those conditions. I had childishly believed that when the drugs were no longer a problem, there would be no problems. Now we had to face the problems that plague all married couples—disciplining the children, dealing with finances, daily living. I had handled those matters alone for so many years; now Bob was taking even those things from me.

"I had prayed so desperately for Bob to change. But now that he was getting well, I became frightened. Bob was drugged when we married. He was drugged throughout most of our relationship. He didn't know me without drugs. Would he still love me? Was he going to need me? Would he be unfaithful again?

"I was depressed; I was insecure; I was jealous; I was demanding; I was manipulative; I was suspicious; I was completely miserable. What was wrong with *me* now? Our marriage took a definite nose dive; we talked about divorce.

"I had set up Bob's new office while he was in Atlanta. I organized the accounting, the purchasing, the charting, the decorating. When he returned, I worked as his assistant when we couldn't afford to hire one, and then finally as his bookkeeper. It was my salvation. It kept me busy, and more importantly, it gave me a chance to keep my eye on Bob. It was *my* office, too.

"Then one day he fired me! After all I had done, he fired me from my own office! He said, 'It's either our marriage or your job. I can always hire office help; but I don't want a new wife.' He said that I was *sick* (I hated that word) and that he would help me as much as he could, but the kingdom of God was within me, too, and I needed to find it. Can you believe that? This man I had prayed for and wept over, this man who almost died from his drug addiction was now telling me I needed help?

"But I had heard it before. While Bob was still using drugs, I had been told by several people to get help for myself. It was suggested that I attend Alanon (the companion organization of AA for families of alcoholics and addicts). I had listened politely and even attended a few token meetings. But I was present in body only. I could not understand how my attending these meetings could possibly help Bob, and I was obsessed with helping him. After all, he was the one who was sick. I didn't feel I had the time and certainly not the energy to put forth effort for myself. I had a baby and two school-age children to care for. The closest meeting was twenty-five miles away, and they had mentioned that I should probably attend several each week. Besides, I felt I was doing extremely well under difficult circumstances. As far as I was concerned, I was doing okay. What did these people expect from me?

"Finally, out of sheer desperation, I began to attend Alanon meetings again. I met with Jim and Dan. This time I knew *I* needed help. I talked with other spouses. I found out my feelings and fears were normal. Not healthy, but normal. Just knowing that others had shared my feelings was comforting. My life had been greatly affected by Bob's disease, as had our children's lives. We would all need treatment to recover.

"For the first time in our marriage, I began to look at my own inadequacies—before I had seen only Bob's. I learned I was not to blame for Bob's addiction; nor could I take any credit for his recovery. Instead of focusing on change, I began to look for growth. My own growth.

"As Bob and I grew individually, our marriage became stronger. We started finding the kingdom of God—together.

"Jim had told Bob that 'something divine, something supernatural' would happen to him. It did. Christ was no longer *just* a great man; to Bob, He was the Son of God. 'I can explain my resurrection no other way,' he said. 'I don't think Lazarus questioned the divinity of Jesus Christ. I don't either.'

"Bob put away his military books and began reading spiritual literature and the Bible (not as much as Dan and Jim wanted him to, however). He read about Peter Marshall who had died at the young age of forty-six of a heart attack. Bob knew that his own life span had been shortened considerably by the damage the drugs had inflicted on his body, but he quoted Marshall, 'The measure of a life, after all, is not its duration but its donation.' He said he wanted to donate, but he didn't know how. 'I guess God's plan for me is just to be alive.' He added, 'I agree with Peter Marshall— it's not the quantity of life that's important, but it's the quality of life. Christ has given me quality living.'

"When he read in the Bible that his body was the temple

of the Holy Spirit, his response was, 'It's a damaged temple, to be sure, but it can still run and exercise.' He started jogging and playing racquetball. He played for months and lost every game. As he said, 'I became mediocre in no time!' But for the first time in his life, he wasn't playing to win. He didn't talk about winning. He didn't need the status anymore.

"Initially, Bob considered prayer similar to eating. 'I say a small one in the morning and a big one at night.' He always started the day by asking God to remove the temptation for drugs and ended the day by thanking God for a drug-free day. Then he read in Thessalonians that we should 'pray without ceasing.' He had always teased me about my 'one-liners' to God. Now he started praying one-liners throughout the day: 'Dear God, don't let me be late for my surgery,' or 'Dear God, don't let it rain on my fishing day.'

"He started praying for his patients. 'I tell them I'm praying for them,' he said. 'Especially before surgery. Whether they're Christian or not, they are comforted by the knowledge that God will guide my hands in the operating room. I used to write orders for a sleeping pill for my patients the night before surgery. Now I tell them I'm praying for them. And you know something? Very few patients need that pill. There is something tranquilizing about knowing that God's on the surgical team.'

"He started touching people—physically touching them and hugging them to let them know he cared about them. He smiled and laughed and looked directly into people's eyes. Bob's recovery, his 'resurrection,' was contagious."

THE BATTLE GOES ON

One Sunday evening, about a year into my recovery, Carolyn and the children and I were driving to church. While Carolyn and the children were talking and laughing together, I was having my own silent conversation.

I had made a practice of using my time in the car for quiet meditation. (Which shows how far God had brought me: from the madman who wished to shoot down any driver who got in his way, I had been transformed into a man who looked forward to the peaceful, relaxing swish of tires as a background for prayer.) Carolyn respected my "God time" and seldom interrupted. But that particular evening, she sensed something was wrong.

"You look troubled," she said. "Are you talking to God?"

"We're arguing."

"Who?"

"God and I."

"Bob! You shouldn't argue with God."

"Why not? He's my best friend. Friends have arguments, don't they? We argue frequently."

"Who wins?"

"Oh, God does. Always. He sends me a mental letter that says:

Dear Bob,

I don't need your will today.

227

Love,
God

and that usually straightens me out. But not this time."

Carolyn laughed. "Tell me about it," she said.

"Well, it all started several months ago when Jim asked me if I thought chemical dependency was a disease . . .

" 'Yes,' I said.

" 'Who does God use to treat diseases?' Jim asked.

" 'Doctors,' I said.

" 'Do you think a diabetic doctor would be a good doctor to treat other diabetics?'

" 'Of course,' I said. 'He would have firsthand knowledge of the disease.'

"Now I wasn't stupid. I knew what Jim was getting at. This was confirmed when he then asked what I thought God's plan for my life was.

" 'I don't know,' I said.

" 'Well, Bob, have you ever thought about why God spared your life? There were so many times you were at the brink of death—the cocaine, the nitrous tank, the Sodium Pentothal.'

" 'I guess it just wasn't my time yet. . . .' "

I told Carolyn that Jim had then said something about my having an insight and knowledge of alcoholism and drug addiction that wasn't printed in the medical textbooks or taught in classrooms. Then he changed the subject, and we never talked about it again.

Not many weeks later, Dan read something to me from Corinthians. Something about "when I am weak, then I am strong." He had mentioned that concept before. He asked if I thought I could ever use my weakness as my strength. I knew what he was talking about, too, but I feigned ignorance. He, too, asked what I thought God's plan for my life was, and I again said I didn't know. Be a good husband and father—maybe a good doctor. Not to use drugs again. I didn't know. I asked him what plan he thought God had for me. He laughed and said, "Only God and you can determine that."

"We haven't talked about it again," I told Carolyn that evening in the car. "But since those conversations, I've had this nagging voice in my mind, God's voice, telling me to help another addict. That's the argument. . . . But Carolyn, I can't even help myself. I live one day at a time. I'm one pill or drink away from killing myself again. I don't have any recoveries left. How does God expect me to help someone else? If that's God's plan for me, if that's why He saved my life—then I want no part of it. Drug addiction is so overpowering. My efforts would be futile. I'd be inviting failure because very few people recover from this madness—"

"You did," Carolyn interrupted. "And remember, God doesn't need your will today."

As Carolyn and I talked that evening, and many successive evenings, about this matter, the old voice would return. *"So you found the way out, huh? Herr General. I never thought you would. But don't think you've won the war. Far from it. The war goes on until the day you die. I'll always be there to haunt you—to tempt you. As you said, you're only one pill or drink away from killing yourself. And believe me, I'll be waiting and watching.*

"But even if you win this war, no big deal. I've got millions just like you under contract to alcohol and drugs. Millions. You're small potatoes. You can tell them the way out all you want to, but they won't listen. They're mine—for eternity."

Perhaps God did have a plan for my life.

You have just read the true narrative of a miracle.

For those of you who believe in the power of Jesus Christ, no explanation is necessary.

For those of you who don't believe in the power of Jesus Christ, no explanation is possible.

Bob Gehring

Christmas, 1983

AFTERWORD

by Dan Griffin

The first night Bob Gehring came to Cliff Temple Baptist Church, he was, by his own admission, "a junkie grabbing at a straw." Before Bob left the church that night, he and Carolyn, Jim and Jan Boyd, and I talked about the necessity of personal counseling. Bob and I set the next day, Monday, December 22, 1980, as his first appointment in my office. Carolyn said she'd come with him.

Since this was my first experience in helping a "real" drug addict, I was nervous and uncertain about how to proceed. We began by seeing each other twice a week. Although Bob scarcely believed it would help to come talk to me, he was willing to try it because (a) he was desperate and (b) Jim Boyd had insisted on it, had predicated his own assistance on whether or not Bob kept his appointments with me.

At our first meeting, Bob was quite emotional. From time to time during our session, his eyes would fill with tears and he'd duck his head with wrenching sobs. I remember vividly his saying that he didn't know if he would live much longer because of the damage he had inflicted on his body. I asked him what he meant. It was then that the story of his real drug abuse began to spill out.

He explained to me the kinds of drugs he had binged on for several years, the residual effects in his respiratory and vascular systems, and his great fear that he couldn't stay

233

away from resuming the active addiction. He told me that his previous sobriety record was only four months and that he had achieved it several times only to break it again and get in a worse mess.

I made a promise to him that was more bravado than assurance. "Bob, no matter what you do, I'm going to stay with you. You're not going to get rid of me simply by taking drugs again. I'm afraid you're stuck with me. In Christ, I love you right now, . . . and nothing can change that." He looked a little stunned, his eyes still red and moist from crying. I continued, "No matter what you do, take drugs again, stop coming to our appointments, quit coming to church—whatever! I'll come find you. I'll dog your trail. I'll come after you and get you. You can't get rid of me!"

To this day I don't know exactly why I said it with such fervor. I'd never said it to anyone else like that. However, he apparently believed me, and thus put himself under the "house arrest" of our personal friendship.

As we would do many times thereafter, we concluded that first session by holding hands—Bob, Carolyn, and I in a little circle—and sharing a prayer I said as honestly and sincerely as I could. We agreed to see each other for an hour twice a week.

What makes a drug addict? The evidence is convincing that alcoholism is a combination of genetics and biochemistry. Doubtless the same composite dynamic prevails in the person disposed to chemical dependence of other kinds. Those factors can readily be seen in Bob Gehring. In his recovery he was told that he was born with the disease of drug addiction—that he was genetically and biochemically predisposed to addiction. The alcohol and pot were just the first steps in the fatal progression of that disease. Of all the men who used heroin in Vietnam, only the true addicts continued their use after returning home. The rest stopped their addiction and led productive lives. Bob couldn't stop—not even with marijuana.

Looking back, the symptoms stand out in bold relief. He

blacked out the first time he drank to excess. Though his parents were teetotalers, there were relatives in his extended family who had problems with alcohol. This history, by itself, should have tipped him off. Though it didn't, Bob's story has a happy ending. He has beaten the odds. Drugs and attendant death have not prevailed this time. But that victory did not come easily.

Bob's progress was slow. Time and time again I thought we'd lose him (*we* being the Lord, Dr. Boyd, Carolyn, and I). He would swing sharply from enthusiastic sprints of growth to the nether gloom of lethal depression.

He came in one day, sullen and angry, and announced bluntly that he was leaving Carolyn. Ironically, his progress out of the pit was putting pressure on their fragile marriage. She had adapted to his dependence and, subconsciously, resisted the restoration of his independence. His successive healing, the peeling back of the clammy grip of addiction, was extricating him from the incarceration adduced by cocaine and Dilaudid. He wanted, *demanded,* the liberty he had so pitifully and quietly surrendered during the days when even answering the telephone was too great a responsibility for him.

Carolyn, having learned to cope with an addict-husband, two half-grown children, and a new baby, was unsure if Bob could ever be trusted again to function responsibly. No one blamed her for being cautious. For years she had made all the major decisions, answered the phone every time it rang, guided the office staff, and kept the books for Bob's practice. Understandably, she found it difficult and painful to suddenly surrender her independence, responsibility, power. The situation was aggravated by Bob's need to see his healing in terms of regained power and independence.

Dr. Boyd, Carolyn, and I bargained with Bob to parcel out a little freedom at a time. He could carry only a certain amount of money. He needed to account for his time. He must assure all of us of his continued abstinence. Until then, we agreed that to give everything back at once might provide more temptation than he could handle in a weak moment. He resisted all these limitations and was restive under their restraint to a degree, but he also understood they were imposed in love and consideration for his continued progress toward wholeness and restoration.

Besides his meetings with Dr. Boyd and myself, Bob was also attending both an AA meeting and an NA (Narcotics Anonymous) meeting weekly. This "massive" counseling was as therapeutic as it was time-consuming. It kept him busy. It kept him in the context of help. He was going to thirteen separate hours of counseling and group experience every week. For months he was punctual and conscientious about this commitment to getting help. If he were going to be late or had to cancel, he would call, without fail, to let us know. He truly cooperated in the saving of his own life.

Bob confessed much later that he only barely believed that coming to me twice a week would really help. However, we quickly formed a friendship—a true friendship. I still can't explain why or how it occurred. And I doubt seriously that Bob could. Neither can I determine, even from this distance, how important that friendship-type of a relationship between minister and addict may be. I only know that it happened and it helped.

Selfishness is the root problem of any addiction, addiction results from wanting that "good feeling" too much. It is pampering ourselves by giving in to the incessant demands of the flesh. It is the child in us that resists maturity and wants to escape continually from responsibility. It's the ego that insists on being catered to and getting its way that drives a person to overindulge—whether it is alcohol, drugs, food, or whatever.

One day when we were talking about Christianity and the church, Bob suddenly blurted out that he wasn't at all sure there was a God. It was then and during subsequent visits that I realized how far we had to go in bringing Bob all the way to Christ. Fortunately, as Bob would say repeatedly later, I didn't "preach" to him.

Often Bob gave evidence of a stubborn refusal or inability to believe even in the *existence* of God. At first this bothered me since he had made a profession of faith in Christ and I had baptized him into the membership of our church. For someone who had gone through all that to insist that he just couldn't believe in God was a bit disconcerting to me to say the least. Carolyn was also puzzled by his failure to affirm the most basic Christian belief. Because he was struggling at this point, he had a great deal of trouble reading the Bible or getting into Bible study.

Bob was basically a deist. He believed that there was a Deity who had created the world. That God had wound up the world like a complicated clock and had left it running while He retreated into the recesses of eternity's "back forty" to meditate or something. But the god Bob believed in was not one who had any real interest in him or any unusual demands or designs for his life. It was the God revealed in the New Testament that Bob found incredible.

Bob had no real faith in Jesus Christ. He believed only in Jim Boyd, as he would later also come to believe in me. But it was faith enough. I've learned over twenty years of pastoring that people—especially people like Bob whose sins and lifestyle have catapulted them way beyond the normal reach of the church—need God *and* another living, breathing human being who can walk with them on the prodigal's journey home.

Bob had joined Cliff Temple, not because it was a fresh, new religious experience or conversion, but simply because Dr. Boyd told him to. At this point Bob would have followed literally any suggestion or directive, clinging as he was, however incredulously, to Jim's promise that, if he'd do whatever Jim told him to, he'd stay alive and whip this beast.

As Bob revealed more and more of himself to me, I realized that we had many things in common. With my own compulsive behavior and tendency to abuse pleasures, he was the person I might well have become had I fulfilled my high-school dream of becoming a medical doctor. Repeatedly I told him, and meant it, that I needed him as a counselee as much or more than he needed me as a counselor.

Like so many people in our society, Bob had bought completely the whole cultural agenda and lifestyle ascribed to one in his professional niche. He had carefully selected obstetrics and gynecology because he couldn't hack oncology or cardiology. He didn't want to deal with dying people all the time. He wanted to be around life and happiness, the kind normally associated with the joy of pregnancy and birth. Moreover, he wanted to be around women.

He chose Baylor Hospital and a North Dallas constituency because he felt the "beautiful people" were his natural bent. He desired a lucrative practice among lovely, affluent women who would be impressed by a tall, dark, handsome, curly-haired M.D. in a crisp white jacket with Dr. W. Robert Gehring stitched in bright-red cursive writing over the pocket bulging with the inevitable pencils, pens, tongue depressors, and cigarettes.

To help Bob, I had, somehow, to get him to study the Bible. I knew that if he would read the Bible, God would reveal Himself sufficiently for Bob's inquiring intellect. But he was working against a great deal of spiritual inertia. Plus, like many church members and all new Christians, he faced the Bible as the great "Unknown Book" that all Christians are supposed to love and understand immediately from the moment of their conversion experience.

My firm conviction is that until a person is in a proper relationship to God, that person cannot get his or her tangled life or problems sorted out. For me that proper relationship involves following Jesus as His disciple. Bob had made a public commitment to Christ by coming down the aisle that Christmas Sunday and then by being baptized. The next step, I explained to him, is the fun part, . . . the adventure, . . . the exciting growth area. But, it's also the part where the hard work comes in—discipleship.

As I talked about discipleship, in great detail over a period of weeks, I could tell from Bob's reaction that I was a long way from securing his active involvement. Even when I described how discipleship leads naturally to apostleship and Christlikeness, the goal of the Christian life, Bob's facial expressions indicated that he was thinking, "This may be well and good for 'normal' people, . . . but I'm a drug addict." (Being a drug addict is just another way for a selfish person to feel, in an inverted way, very special again.)

As Bob stabilized, he began seeking more and more independence. Ultimately, we succumbed to his pleading and took him out of "intensive care" precipitously. With the renewed freedom, he actually regressed and took drugs again a couple of times.

Although I had described the "intensive care" of the Holy Spirit to Bob as the constant affirmation and concern he could depend on receiving from me, the Boyds, and the church, I don't think he really accepted the fact that our care of him would be *durable,* . . . that he could reject us but we would never reject him.

In spite of our constant assurances, he hid his lapses from us like a little boy with jam on his face. Carolyn would come and tell me, or Jim Boyd would call to say he was suspicious that Bob had been on drugs again.

One particular Saturday, I noticed that Bob was especially nervous and restive. He could hardly sit still in my office. His answers were abrupt, and superficial, unlike his normal serious involvement, as though he was struggling with some inner distraction. He was in a hurry to conclude our meeting and leave.

Several weeks passed before he confessed to me that he had taken drugs again—three times! I assured him that I was proud of him for having the courage to face up to his failure and confess it and that his relapse would not drive a wedge between us.

I'm not naive enough to think that every drug addict can succeed as Bob did. He is a very intelligent person who, in spite of his serious addiction, never surrendered his brain to drugs nor convinced himself that his various deceptions, effected in order to take drugs, were true. He was very much aware of the enemy he was dealing with.

After he confessed to me that he had slipped several times, we discussed how the temptation came and the grave danger it posed to his ultimate recovery. He promised that he would be honest and tell me if the pressure started building up again—and he did. Now he had someone with whom he could share that private hell of temptation— someone who wouldn't condemn him for being human and vulnerable to the raging physical thermostat that, both congenitally and through years of chemical abuse, was set to call incessantly for more. Changing the setting on the thermostat was the name of the game. A surgeon can go through the stomach to remove a tumor, but how do you excise a hunger? Only through the head. To make a psychological incision without killing the patient is a delicate operation and requires God's powerful assistance.

The part God and our mutual Christian faith consistently played in Bob's physical salvation cannot be overestimated. Christian help moves on legs of love. I had truly learned to love Bob and Carolyn. Jesus, our Brother, ministered to us through our love for each other, a love that would not have been there had He not been there.

Bob's exceptional recovery may have come about in large part because of who he is, which prepared him to respond to Jim Boyd and myself. Drug addiction is too resistant to therapy for us to opine casually that any counselor-patient relationship should follow the basic dy- namics and game plan ours did. However, we do acknowl- edge God's strong leadership throughout the process.

As I talked with Bob week after week, I began to see that he should share the victory he was experiencing. His first public testimony, quite appropriately, was from the pulpit of the Cliff Temple Baptist Church in Dallas. Appropriate because it was now *his* church family he was addressing. At times during that testimony his voice was barely audible. He broke off weeping several times, as when he admitted, "I was a dead man . . ."

Telling of his emergence from addiction seemed to exhilarate Bob, and he began to look for opportunities to relate his experiences, discovering each time he did that it gave him new strength and drew other closet-addicts to seek him out for help. He proved to be a spellbinding speaker, and audiences were impressed with the courage it took for this doctor still in private practice to speak out about his drug addiction.

As the weeks and months flew by, Bob's practice began to build again. Ironically, many new patients came because they saw him on TV or read one of the many news articles about him. Those patients in turn referred their friends to him.

Those women who not only had need of a good gynecologist but were also taking drugs came to a Tuesday afternoon group meeting he had started. Many men came also. Bob gave me a standing invitation to join them on Tuesdays at 5:00 P.M. whenever I could. When I was able to go, I was always impressed with Bob's empathy but firm hand and advice for those who ventured to admit addiction, tell their whole stories, and seek healing in the small group process. Some drifted in and out; others came faithfully every week and held on to the two-hour sessions of sharing as if they were the umbilical to life. It is no exaggeration to say that scores of lives have been saved by this one aspect of Bob's total rehabilitation. He needed to help in order to heal; they needed his help in order to live.

Finally, Bob gradually learned to stop feeling responsible for either medical victories or defeats. About a year after he began meeting with me, he delivered twins, one dead and one alive. It truly bothered and depressed him; he wanted to feel guilty about it. We talked about it at length.

He even joked about his seemingly insatiable need to heap guilt upon himself. "Got a truckload of guilt? Come dump it on me! I can use it to rationalize my drug addiction. Load me up!"

Release came hard, because to release himself from stillbirths or other gynecological abnormalities, he also had to give up the godlike elation that he'd always derived from a victory. And that exhilaration had been as heady as cocaine. Eventually he accepted it as a good trade-off: he was no pseudodeity, but neither was he a butter-fingered failure!

Few people ever recover from drug addiction, especially when they've been as deeply into it as Bob Gehring was. But through Christ, all things are possible. All I had to share with Bob was my faith in Christ. That's all Jim Boyd had, too. Yet Christ uses His followers to continue His healing ministry on earth.

FURTHER INFORMATION

DOCTORS HELPING DOCTORS

The American Medical Association defines an impaired physician as "one who is unable to practice medicine with reasonable skill and safety to patients because of physical or mental illness, including deterioration through the aging process or loss of motor skill, or excessive use or abuse of drugs including alcohol."

Many impaired physicians are reluctant to seek help because they deny that a problem exists (alcoholism is called a "disease of denial.") Even if they are aware of the problem, they minimize its seriousness. They are afraid of the stigma attached to the odious admission of drug addiction. They fear malpractice suits, criminal charges (illegal prescriptions), loss of hospital privileges, income, and reputation. The wounded healer is slow to seek healing.

Where do doctors go when they are sick? Who can penetrate their enormous intellectual defenses and convince them of the positive alternative to drinking and drugging? Usually, only other doctors.

Following the concept of doctors helping other doctors, and based on the success of the Caduceus Club in Atlanta, Georgia, four Dallas physicians met anonymously in March of 1979 to help each other recover from the madness of their addictions. They borrowed heavily from the tenets of Alcoholics Anonymous, stressing the spiritual aspect of recovery. *God, as we understand Him* became the corner-stone of the program.

From these humble beginnings, the Dallas group has grown to over sixty recovering addicts. *Doctors Helping Doctors* has chapters in eight major cities in Texas, and groups are being organized nationwide. Meetings are held weekly to discuss common problems, share positive experiences, and instill hope—especially to the newcomer. The meeting ends with the Lord's Prayer and the admonishment, "Keep coming back; it works!"

EARLY CASE-FINDING— ALCOHOLISM AND DRUG DEPENDENCE

by G. Douglas Talbott, M.D.

Impaired physicians are present in large numbers, but it is often difficult to identify a physician who is ill because he may have long since dropped out of professional medical circles.

There are a number of reasons besides the impaired physician's isolation that make case-finding difficult. These include the physician's depression, guilt, anger, and fear. The impaired physician also is unable to reach out for help because of self-deception, which is a basic component of the disease of chemical dependence, and because of denial, which is inherent not only in every physician who is ill but among family members and colleagues as well. Personal, family, and professional pride deters many physicians from getting the help they need.

When discussing the need for early case-finding, it's important to emphasize and understand the nature of impairment, a sequential progression of deterioration that occurs in the following major areas of a physician's life:

- community involvement
- family life
- job application
- health and physical status
- office conduct
- behavior in the hospital

247

By the time the impairment is noticeable in the office or the hospital, the illness is usually quite advanced. The physician who is impaired peels off—like the skin of an onion—successive activities: first, the community; second, the church; third, peers; fourth, partners; fifth, distant family; and sixth, the nuclear family.

To aid in the early identification process, the Medical Association of Georgia has developed the following list of characteristic behaviors in the major areas of a physician's life that may signal actual impairment or impending trouble. Using these six areas of the check list, talk to family and community members, review job applications, and assess the health of your peers, including behavior and performance in the office. If you do this, early case-finding is possible. Don't wait for publicity of disciplinary action to appear on the front page of your local paper or on the evening TV news.

The earlier impairment is identified, the sooner treatment can begin and the better the physician's chances are for complete recovery and return to practice.

Clues to alcoholism or drug addiction in six areas of a physician's life*

Community

Isolation and withdrawal from community activities, leisure activities and hobbies, church, friends, peers
Embarrassing behavior at clubs or parties
Arrests for driving while intoxicated, legal problems
Unreliability and unpredictability in community and social activities
Unpredictable behavior, e.g., inappropriate spending, excessive involvement in political activities

---

*Areas are usually involved sequentially, although two or three may seem to be involved simultaneously.

Family

Withdrawal from family activities, unexplained absences from home
Fights, child abuse
Development in spouse of disease of "spouse-aholism'
Abnormal, antisocial, illegal behavior by children
Sexual problems—impotence, extramarital affairs, contra-cultural sexual behavior
Assumption of surrogate role by spouse and children
Institution of geographic separation or divorce proceedings by spouse

Employment

Numerous job changes in past five years
Frequent geographic relocations for unexplained reasons
Frequent hospitalizations†
Complicated and elaborate medical history†
Unexplained intervals between jobs
Indefinite or inappropriate references
Working in job inappropriate for qualifications
Reluctance of job applicant to let spouse and children be interviewed
Reluctance to undergo immediate preemployment physical examination

Physical status

Deterioration in personal hygiene
Deterioration in clothing and dressing habits
Multiple physical signs and complaints
Numerous prescriptions and drugs
Frequent hospitalizations
Frequent visits to physicians and dentists
Accidents
Emotional crises

---

†Information obtained from employment applications.

Office

Disruption of appointment schedule
Hostile, withdrawn, unreasonable behavior to staff and
    patients
"Locked-door syndrome"
Excessive ordering of supplies of drugs from local druggists
    or by mail
Complaints by patients to staff about doctor's behavior
Absence from office—unexplained or due to frequent illness

Hospital

Making rounds late, or inappropriate, abnormal behavior
    during rounds
Decreasing quality of performance, e.g., in staff presenta-
    tions, writing in chart
Inappropriate orders or overprescription of medications
Reports of behavioral changes from hospital personnel
    ("hospital gossip")
Involvement in malpractice suits and legal sanctions against
    hospital
Reports from emergency department staff of unavailability
    or inappropriate responses to telephone calls

Reprinted by permission of G. Douglas Talbott, M.D.,
F.A.C.D.